© Developmental Press
The Cultural & Developmental Institute
240 Argo Avenue
San Antonio, Texas 78209

The Cross-Age Mentoring Program (CAMP) for Children with Adolescent Mentors:
Program Manual

Developed by Michael J. Karcher, Ed.D., Ph.D.

Cover photos from CAMP (Columbus, Wisconsin, 1999)
and Velocity (San Antonio, TX 2012) with written consent

ISBN: 0-9774373-2-9

10 9 8 7 6 5 4 3 2 1
Printed in the United States of America

Acknowledgements:

The Columbus, Wisconsin School District; Brad Powell, Rev. Pat Gahan, and The St. Stephen's Episcopal School in Austin, Texas; The Boy with a Ball staff who conduct the "Velocity" program in Harlandale ISD, San Antonio, Texas.

Michael Garringer, Eve McDermott, Patty McCrae, Amy Cannata, and Nicky Martin at the National Mentoring Center, Education Northwest, Portland Oregon.

Ben Judson

CONTENTS

INTRODUCTION: THE POWER OF PEER MENTORING

Welcome to the Cross-Age Mentoring Program (CAMP). CAMP is a powerful peer mentoring model that can have a meaningful impact on the young people who participate, as well as on their schools, families, and communities. This program manual provides the basic information you will need to start a CAMP in your school. It is designed to work in concert with the *CAMP Mentor Training Guide,* which details training for older peer mentors, and the *CAMP Connectedness Curriculum,* which is packed with ideas for fun and meaningful activities for mentor and mentee matches that target key program outcomes described in this manual.

What is CAMP?

CAMP is a structured developmental cross-age peer mentoring program. It was developed by Dr. Michael Karcher at the University of Texas–San Antonio, one of the leading experts and researchers in the youth mentoring field. His goal was to create a developmental intervention built upon several prominent youth development theories and the programmatic structures necessary to produce positive impacts for all students who participate.

The program matches high school peer mentors with mentees in elementary or middle school. The matches primarily meet after school at the mentees' campus, but quarterly weekend meetings including parents are involved, and an optional summer component can be included by programs that wish to provide CAMP activities year round.

As with adult mentors, cross-age peer mentors provide the younger student with guidance, social support, and *limited* academic assistance. However, teen mentors have special needs. Unlike adult mentors, teen mentors must be provided with more training, supervision, and support to promote effective interactions with their younger mentees. For this reason, the mentor and mentee typically meet within a larger peer group context in which planned dyadic (and some group) activities can be coordinated and supervised by program staff.

A unique element of CAMP—and what distinguishes it from peer tutoring, counseling, and helping— is that the program serves more to promote self-development, social and cognitive development than to achieve specific academic, behavioral, or other specified goals. It is intended to help students grow as individuals rather than master a skill or solve some specific problem.

CAMP Mission Statement

The mission of CAMP is to nurture responsibility, leadership, and social interest among teens for their school and community by supporting them in the role of peer mentors. These personal characteristics can help foster the teen mentors' own social, emotional, and academic development while, in turn, they support the developmental growth of their mentees: younger children in their community, some of whom are at risk for underachievement and social problems, as well as many others who simply may benefit from entering into positive peer relationships.

CAMP Vision Statement

CAMP views all youth as having the potential to be primary agents of one another's and their community's development. The program should be led by adults who believe that (a) nurturing one-to-one relationships between teens and children can help both develop their full potential and (b) youth are capable of making informed, responsible decisions as involved members of the community.

The reason we define CAMP as developmental mentoring is that the program serves to foster emotional, social and cognitive development. Emotional development is promoted by serving two important psychodynamic developmental needs:

1. The need for empathy, praise, and attention
2. The need for a consistent, competent, and clearly supportive role model

How do peer mentors and mentees help each other develop?

One of the most appealing attributes of the CAMP model is that it cultivates positive outcomes for both the younger mentees and their older peer mentors. This dual impact is facilitated by CAMP's use of key components from theories on child development, psychology, and education as a basis for program structure and activities.

1. Erikson's Stages of Development

CAMP provides youth with developmentally appropriate roles by affording them several social and self-development opportunities throughout their time in the program. Both observational learning and the processes of modeling, as well as the experience of enhanced social support (that allows for self-definition to occur) through key roles youth play in CAMP:

- Mentees learn about their own unique skills and social norms for interacting

- Mentors practice the use of complex perspective-taking skills and engage in prosocial helping behaviors that can directly shape their developing identity

- Lead Mentors are able to take on leadership roles, model problem solving, and practice other advanced interpersonal skills that can help them in their later career and personal relationships

To ensure that CAMP provides these roles, a set of sequential curriculum activities are used, each of which reflects an opportunity for self-development. These activities are based on the idea that self-development is an exploration not only of who one is but of how one is experienced in relationships with others. The CAMP curriculum addresses these needs by providing a relational context and a structured role for both mentors and mentees.

2. Connectedness

Each opportunity for self-development or self-definition is the result of the experience of connectedness. Connectedness reflects our emotional and physical engagement with others, the environment, and our own sense of self in the present and future. Because how we understand ourselves, others, and the future changes with cognitive development, the nature of connectedness changes between childhood and adulthood (and continues to evolve across the adult lifespan). Developmental experiences of connectedness start with infant/child bonding and culminate in connections to society and history experienced by the elderly.

Even in the later elementary and middle school years there are important differences among pre-, early- and late-adolescents in how they experience connectedness, which are elaborated more fully in Chapter 5. CAMP is built on the premise that intergenerational contact allows youth of varying ages to assist each other in forging the kinds of connections that are most important to each other's current stage of development.

The mentor's and mentee's time together is structured to encourage them to participate in activities that match their developmental abilities and subsequently help them become more connected to their teachers, families, communities, and futures. It is our hope and expectation that the activities that form the basis of their CAMP interactions—those described in the CAMP Connectedness

Curriculum—should help the mentees manage and improve their connections to important people and places in their ever-widening social ecology.

3. Perspective taking

The important connections individuals need to establish throughout their life are shaped by their cognitive development, generally, and more specifically by their capacity to coordinate social perspectives. Social perspective taking is the ability to understand the thoughts and ideas of others and the meaning one makes in experiences of negotiating other perspectives and our own. CAMP uses a model of social development to structure the activities so that they encourage youth to learn more complex interpersonal negotiation and perspective-taking skills.

CAMP lets mentors and mentees practice and refine a range of perspective-based social skills in a fun, safe, and supportive environment. Some of the structured interactions presented in the *CAMP Connectedness Curriculum* (Karcher & Judson, 2012), such as the icebreaker activities, may seem quite playful (even directionless), but they are in fact both purposeful and essential as revealed in developmental perspective-taking theory (Selman, 1980). For example, the curriculum may suggest the mentor and mentee play games together and talk about events that happened in the prior week. However, it follows this "catching up" time of sharing separate, individual perspectives with collaborative activities that help their newly emergent social skills take hold and become more readily available for use in other social interactions in their daily lives. The mentees learn how to cooperate and compromise by negotiating their needs and relating one another's experiences, while the mentors learn to take a perspective on their relationship, to see the power of collaboration and social interest in close relationships.

Youth who are struggling socially and academically often do not engage in age-appropriate social behaviors. Consequently, the program is designed to regularly walk the mentees through each of the developmental stages in perspective taking. This provides mentees with practice in both the perspective-taking skills they should have mastered already as well as skills that they and their peers are currently trying to master. We call this process "walking the youth up the developmental ladder," and we describe the theory behind it later in this manual.

What can CAMP achieve for participants?

What interests people most about CAMP is that it is designed to help youth become more connected to their teachers, families, communities, and to their own futures. This increased connectedness, in turn, can lead to other positive outcomes as the mentees (and their mentors) bring their newly developed social skills, perspectives, and attitudes to the other areas of their lives.

Research on CAMP has consistently found that mentees demonstrate improvements in:

- Connectedness to school and peers
- Academic interest and achievement
- Social skills
- Behavior problems
- Conventional attitudes toward illicit and antisocial behavior (see Karcher, 2007 for full citations)

These improvements can help mentees become more resilient against peer pressure and the other challenges they face as they enter into and navigate adolescence. Strengthened relationships with teachers and parents will bolster mentees' interest and efforts in academic success. Program participants are more likely to develop mature and satisfying relationships with peers and friends, and less likely to engage in negative behaviors in school and other social contexts.

There is more limited evidence of CAMP's effect on *mentors,* but the research available suggests involvement in CAMP is positively associated with higher ratings of academic connectedness and self-esteem compared to youth not serving as CAMP mentors (Karcher, 2009). However, there is considerable evidence of the benefits of serving as a peer mentor. A randomized study of 129 high school students found improvements in moral reasoning and empathy after youth served as peer mentors (Ikard, 2001). Another study reported that "a positive experience with the peer mentoring program was predictive of a more favorable connection to school" (Stoltz, 2006, p. 11). Similarly, in one evaluation of the Big Brothers Big Sisters High School (HS Bigs) program, "The HS Bigs felt mentoring helped them to improve their ability to communicate with children, to become more responsible, to forge a stronger connection to their community and school" (Hansen, 2006, p. 3).

About this manual

This manual walks you through the process of planning, implementing, and refining a CAMP in your school. No two CAMPs will look exactly the same, as local contextual factors result in modifications to the model. Therefore, the guidance in this manual is designed to be general and flexible. You will find many self-assessment questions and other prompts intended to get you thinking about how CAMP can be customized to meet your students' needs.

While there is plenty of room for variation in the CAMP model, two things are critical in order to maintain the integrity of the program. You must have complete buy-in at the participating schools, and mentor-mentee activities must provide opportunities to build connectedness in a way that is developmentally appropriate for each participant.

CHAPTER 1. OVERVIEW OF THE CAMP MODEL

This chapter provides a general overview of CAMP, built around a set of "frequently asked questions" about the program. You may find the content of this chapter useful in summarizing CAMP for teachers, funders, or other stakeholders.

Who typically implements CAMP?

A CAMP is most often implemented by schools or districts wanting to improve the social, emotional, and personal development of their students. CAMPs do not necessarily target at-risk students or struggling schools. In fact, a CAMP works best when it serves a diverse set of students at a school that is neither exemplary nor dealing with severe institutional problems. The model is often selected by schools or districts wanting a broad-based supplemental support program that can enhance students' connectedness and well-being.

A Program Coordinator oversees the CAMP. This role may be filled by a counselor, teacher, or other adult who has the time available to effectively manage the program. Schools may decide to contract with an external mentoring provider to implement the program on site.

Regardless of the configuration, each CAMP is a partnership between the mentors' school and the mentees' school. Both schools provide a liaison responsible for working with the Program Coordinator to make the program a reality. Additional information about staffing and leading a CAMP is provided in Chapters 2 and 3.

Who participates in CAMP?

There are three main groups of students who participate in CAMP:

- **Mentees.** These are the younger students who attend the host school. They are typically in grades 4–8 as that is the age when students are best able to participate in and benefit from CAMP activities. These activities are appropriate for both successful and at-risk students. (CAMP may be less appropriate for students with severe emotional or behavioral problems.)

- **Mentors.** Mentors are traditionally high school freshmen, sophomores, and juniors at the partner school. Seniors do not traditionally serve as first-time mentors, as one of the goals of CAMP is multiyear matches. CAMP mentors do not need to possess any special skills or abilities, although certain personality traits contribute to being an effective CAMP mentor (see Chapter 4). Most important, CAMP mentors simply need to have the available time and motivation to participate. Some high schools choose to have mentors participate for credit in a class that has a service-learning component. But, mentor participation can also be purely voluntary as well.

- **Lead Mentors.** Lead Mentors are high school students—often seniors—who have served as a mentor in the past and seek a leadership role in the program. Lead Mentors support the program by facilitating curriculum activities; supervising and assisting the mentors; helping the Program Coordinator change and adapt the program over time; and generally serving as a liaison between the participating youth and the adult leadership. This role is critical in completing the "developmental" aspect of CAMP, as we hope that youth gradually move through the roles of mentee, mentor, and Lead Mentor.

When and where do matches meet?

The most common format for delivering CAMP is the cross-campus model, which has mentors travelling to the mentees' campus after school. Mentoring sessions are typically conducted once a week and last approximately two hours. However, the length can vary depending on the curriculum activities used on a particular day. Some CAMPs conduct the sessions during the school day (especially if the mentors are taking a formal class that includes the mentoring time), but most CAMPs find that after school works well and avoids disrupting students' class schedules. These meetings begin early in the school year, but only after the mentors have received their orientation and initial training. Some of the initial sessions facilitate the students getting to know each other before the mentor-mentee matches are made.

In addition to weekly meetings, CAMP employs half-day events called SuperSaturdays. These events take place every other month, with the primary goal of involving parents of mentees and mentors in the program. SuperSaturday events occur at the school site or at another community location if a group outing is planned, such as a picnic in a park or a trip to a museum. Such events give parents a chance to meet their child's mentor or mentee, see what types of activities they engage in, and talk about the program with the coordinator and other staff.

Sample content and activities for the meetings and SuperSaturdays are provided in Chapter 6. For ambitious programs, there is also an optional summer program component. Additional information about this component can also be found in Chapter 6.

What do matches do together?

All CAMP meetings follow the same basic format, whether held after school or as part of a SuperSaturday. The meetings begin with a group icebreaker, a fun game or activity that gets participants talking. Then, the mentoring pairs meet individually to share their experiences since the last meeting. This built-in bonding time, known as 3-2-1 Reflection, reconnects both participants and lays the foundation for their cooperation during the meeting's main activities.

The pair then moves on to Listen and Learn time, where they work on *Connectedness Curriculum* activities. This is considered the main aspect of the meeting. The curriculum itself is divided into themes that promote connectedness to a particular "world," such as family, school, peers, friends, self, or reading. Each activity engages the pair in a fun and challenging task that gets them thinking and problem solving, followed by an exercise where the mentor and mentee collaborate and share their results with the group. Programs usually offer a snack at the midpoint of this activity, so that participants can keep their energy up.

While the curriculum is used to structure the meeting, the *relationship* between the two participants is most important. The curriculum is designed to be flexible and often is adapted considerably by the mentors themselves to ensure the activities mesh with the youth culture and to gain participants' buy-in. Listen and Learn time ends with a chance for the pair to reflect on the day and start saying goodbye for the week.

The last few minutes of the session are usually spent on an enjoyable group game or activity (e.g., doing artwork or playing basketball). This flexible play time can be interrupted or extended and morphed into different groups to accommodate departure times.

We call this prescribed sequence of activities—from introductions and sharing to purposeful connectedness building to a positive goodbye—"walking the match up the developmental ladder." It is one of the main ways that CAMP incorporates a developmental focus.

How will we know if CAMP is working?

Several evaluation components are built into CAMP to let you know how mentees and mentors are developing throughout the program. The primary evaluation instrument is the *Hemingway Assessment of Adolescent Connectedness,* which is given pre/post to gauge participants' sense of connectedness to a variety of domains. CAMP also uses other instruments, such as a self-esteem scale and a scale of social interest/skills to gauge participant development. These surveys are aligned with the goals and activities of CAMP and have been validated with field use. In addition to these outcome-driven measures, CAMP is also proactive in assessing mentor-mentee relationship quality. Matches that are not close, or are distracted by an issue or conflict, cannot get the most out of the program. By measuring the quality of the mentoring relationships at various points, the Program Coordinator can make needed adjustments to improve the program's results.

Appendix C of this manual provides a number of evaluation forms that elicit participant satisfaction and feedback, allowing you to gather the opinions of teachers, parents, and others about the program's effectiveness.

Over time, you will know that CAMP is working when you see positive changes in the overall culture of the participating schools and in the long-term academic and personal development of those who participate.

What resources are needed to run a program?

As noted earlier, CAMP can be modified and implemented in a variety of ways depending on the available resources. But, there are certain core components that are integral to the success of CAMP:

- **Program Coordinator.** This position is critical and sites should find a way to fund it sustainably.

- **Space for program activities.** This applies not only to the afterschool meetings but also to SuperSaturdays and other program functions, such as mentor training.

- **Reliable transportation to and from program events.** Since CAMP is essentially a cross-campus program, transportation is a critical component. If it is a barrier to involvement and participation, the program will struggle.

- **Other CAMP resources.** While this manual explains program philosophy and start-up, the majority of CAMP activities are found in the *CAMP Mentor Training Guide* and the *CAMP Connectedness Curriculum* (Karcher & Judson, in press). These resources will guide the program throughout the school year.

- **Some modest funds for group activities and events.** Almost all *Connectedness Curriculum* activities can be implemented at little to no cost (e.g., producing handouts, using basic supplies). But, you should also plan some special group activities as part of SuperSaturdays or other kick-off or year-end celebrations. Field trips to the zoo, a fair, or a miniature golf course can be fun ways to enhance the CAMP experience.

- **Commitment to the goals of CAMP.** This component is not financial or structural, but philosophical. One of the common pitfalls for supplemental in-school programming is disagreement among stakeholders about the purpose and goals of the program. Teachers often want a program that solves classroom misbehavior. Principals and administrators may envision improved test scores. Parents might expect homework help or tutoring. Even participating students can have different perceptions about why they are in the program and what they are supposed to be doing. Successful CAMPs have wide agreement on the goals they want to achieve. Stakeholders are in consensus around what connectedness domains they want to focus on and understand what CAMP is and is not within the context of the other supports offered by the school. If all stakeholders commit to a common vision for their CAMP, then the stage is set for long-term success.

The next chapter provides much more detail about the planning and implementation of a new CAMP, including required resources and decisions needed to lay the groundwork for the program.

The following page provides a simple overview of the CAMP model, including all its components. There are self-assessment questions at the end of Chapter 2 that mirror these components and can help you determine how your schools and staff will build the infrastructure of the program.

CHAPTER 2. PREPARING TO IMPLEMENT CAMP

While CAMP is certainly not a complex model, there are many tasks that need to be completed before a program can launch. This chapter summarizes the factors to consider when first starting a CAMP and ends with a set of self-assessment questions that can help guide your program planning efforts.

Getting participating schools on board

As noted previously, the first step in developing a program is securing the buy-in of the participating schools' leadership. Often, this task is handled by someone at the district level who begins the dialogue between the principals of the proposed schools. In other instances, CAMPs have been initiated by the leader at one school, who then starts building a relationship with the partner school. Occasionally, a CAMP will be initiated by a nonprofit or other third party who thinks two local schools would be a good fit for the model.

Program Infrastructure
- Participating schools
- Meeting space
- Budget and resources
- Transportation
- Partnerships

Program Theory
- Connectedness
- Perspective taking
- Developmental stages ("walking the ladder")
- Praise, empathy, and attention
- Theoretically Evolving Activities in Mentoring (TEAM) framework

Program Staffing
- Program Coordinator
- School liaisons
- Administrative support

Participants
- Mentors
- Lead Mentors
- Mentees
- Parents

Meetings and Activities
- After school
- SuperSaturdays
- Summer program (optional)

  Key CAMP activities:
  - Meet-and-Greet matching
  - 3-2-1 Reflection
  - Match Termination Ritual

Training and Supervision
- Prematch training
- Ongoing training
- *CAMP Mentor Training Guide*
- *CAMP Connectedness Curriculum*
- Supporting and recognizing participants

Connectedness Curriculum
- School-year activities
- Summer activities
- Adaptations over time (adults and youth partnership)

Program Evaluation
- Logic models
- *Hemingway Assessment of Adolescent Connectedness*
- Formative and process evaluation

Regardless of where the idea for your CAMP first originated, the program is going to quickly need to establish an advisory committee to take responsibility for the initial planning of the program. This committee should initially include, but not be limited to:

- A representative of the school district
- Principals or other designated leadership from participating schools
- Teachers or counselors at the participating schools
- A representative from the PTA or other parent-involvement organization
- The Program Coordinator and school-site liaisons

The early focus of this group is program planning and implementation. Once the program is established, other members—such as mentors and mentees, parents of participants, other school personnel, and community partners—can join to work on program improvement and sustainability.

The members of the advisory committee must understand the connectedness goals and developmental philosophy of CAMP. More important, they must understand the challenge of operating a quality program and make a long-term commitment to it. There is considerable evidence from the mentoring literature that poorly run mentoring programs produce less-than-optimal mentoring relationships, and that a negative mentoring experience can, in fact, be quite damaging to a young person. There is also strong evidence from the study of peer-led interventions that poorly structured and supervised programs can result in the reinforcement of negative behaviors and contribute to increased delinquency (Dodge, Dishion, & Lansford, 2006), which is one reason all CAMP evaluations should include a measure of delinquent behavior to monitor this possibility.

Cultivating community partners

Depending on the scope and staffing of your CAMP, you may wish to bring in community partners that can provide valuable services, resources, or even assistance in running the program. As mentioned previously, some CAMPs are led by a third-party nonprofit mentoring organization (e.g., Big Brothers Big Sisters) working with the participating schools. But, even if your program is staffed by school personnel, there are many things that community partners can provide:

- Access to fun group activities for mentors and mentees—especially during SuperSaturday events
- In-kind donations of supplies for mentor-mentee projects
- Trainers to cover special areas of youth development or to work with parents
- Volunteers to help with activities such as managing SuperSaturday events or group field trips
- Goods or services that can be used as rewards for mentors or mentees
- Access to funding to keep CAMP thriving over time

Work with your advisory committee to identify potential community partners and the resources they can provide to strengthen your CAMP.

Building the CAMP infrastructure

Once you have the participating schools and community partners on board and an established advisory committee to guide the launch of the program, it's time to start building the day-to-day infrastructure that makes a CAMP function.

Securing meeting space for matches. Providing CAMP matches with an appropriate meeting space is critical. Ideally, matches will meet at the host school in the gymnasium, cafeteria, library, or a classroom—any physical space that can comfortably hold your number of participants and allow for some freedom of movement during activities. Securing a workable space can be complicated, especially if there is another afterschool program operating at the school. End-of-day activities such as sports team practices can also complicate the availability of resources and space during the CAMP meeting time. Work with administrators to figure out where matches can meet.

Many *CAMP Connectedness Curriculum* activities have the mentor-mentee pairs moving around the campus to interview teachers, work on projects in the library, or otherwise make use of the school's resources. Clarify up front when and where mentors will meet with their mentee, what parts of the building they can access, and which school personnel (e.g., teachers, librarians, and coaches) can facilitate use of the school resources and facilities.

Setting a budget. There is no set amount of funding required to run an effective program. As noted earlier, many *CAMP Connectedness Curriculum* activities are free or low cost, but there will still be some costs associated with the weekly match activities and SuperSaturdays.

A CAMP budget will be influenced by many contextual factors, such as the available resources, the configuration of the school staff, and even the city where the program operates. But, your initial budget does need to be able to cover:

- Staff costs, especially the Program Coordinator position
- The cost of space or supplies for meeting activities
- Transportation for participants
- Supplemental pay for teachers or other school staff who assist the program
- Costs associated with SuperSaturday events and field trips
- Food, drinks, and other snacks
- Art supplies
- Administrative costs
- Funds for program evaluation
- Printing of materials (including copies of the *CAMP Mentor Training Guide*, handouts, and activity sheets)

Take some time to go through the curriculum early in the planning process to decide which connectedness domains you want to focus on throughout the year and the resources needed to do so. Also think about supplementary activities, such as field trips or end-of-year recognition ceremonies, which may require some expenditure of resources.

CAMPs are designed to be long-term youth development projects, not a one-time service. Think about long-term sustainability when calculating just how much CAMP will cost and how likely you are to find those funds. Are some of the start-up expenditures a one-time cost or will they be included in every annual budget? Are there potential partnerships or new resources that can supplement your budget over time? What is the minimum funding that the program needs to survive over time?

Arranging for youth transportation. Mentors must be able to get to the host school for the meetings with their mentees. Transportation issues that result in missed meetings can be hurtful to the elementary student, disappointing to the mentor, and problematic for your program goals.

Most programs have participating schools that are close enough so that the mentors can either walk or take a bus to the mentees' school. Mentors and their parents typically find transportation home at the end of the mentoring session. Some CAMPs have chosen to bus the high school students back to their own campus when the session is over, but we've found that it works best to allow the high school students to find their own transportation options at the end of the day.

Staffing the program. Programs can be staffed and structured in many ways, but there are some key roles that need to be filled:

- Program Coordinator. This individual is responsible for all aspects of the program.

- School-site liaisons. These staff members get youth to the participating sites and provide general supervision of the mentoring sessions.

- Teachers and counselors. These positions do not play a major role in CAMP, but they do contribute to some curricular activities and can help support other aspects of the program.

- Evaluator. Most of the evaluation instruments provided with CAMP can be administered by the Program Coordinator, although some CAMPs choose to have an external evaluator who works with them on data analysis and dissemination of evaluation results.

More information about these roles and responsibilities can be found in the next chapter.

The Program Coordinator position is the most critical. Although the duties of the Coordinator are described more fully later in the manual, it is critical to underscore at this point that part of program infrastructure is getting buy-in from administration or agency staff to fully fund and support this position. Running a CAMP is much more time intensive than running an adult-with-youth, in-school mentoring program. In our experience, this role requires at least 20 hours per week. Program Coordinator responsibilities should not be added to the plate of a classroom teacher or school counselor unless that person has at least .5 FTE available to manage the program. For CAMP to be successful, it needs strong leadership and attention to detail, neither of which will be provided if CAMP is an afterthought for an already busy faculty member.

Moving toward implementation

After the advisory committee has worked through these initial planning considerations, it's time to start moving toward the launch of the program. There are several tasks that the committee can focus on before the program officially begins:

- **Create a Memorandum of Understanding (MOU) for participating schools and organizations.** Each participating school (or nonprofit) will have roles and responsibilities it must meet to make the program a success. Putting these agreements in writing is critical, especially if there are changes in leadership or eventual questions about the completion of program tasks. A sample MOU can be found in Appendix B.

- **Develop a policy and procedure manual.** This should be one of your Program Coordinator's first tasks. A policy and procedure manual governs all aspects of the CAMP. The policies clarify things such as mentor eligibility, participant transportation, provision of training and match supervision, and guidelines for participation in the program. The procedures will detail the day-to-day operations of the program, such as how mentors are accepted into the program; how the staff communicates with parents or other stakeholders; and how the Program Coordinator works with Lead Mentors, teachers, and others to implement the program. Sample policies can be found in Appendix B. Day-to-day procedures should be developed based on what will work best at your local site.

- **Set a time line.** Most CAMPs begin enrolling students in the fall when the school year starts. However, the groundwork for launching the program must be laid far in advance. We recommend starting the planning process in the spring of the previous school year, and using the summer break to identify a Program Coordinator and get everything set for the beginning of the new school year. Ambitious programs can even do a "soft launch" at the end of the school year—orienting students and parents to the program and getting participants excited about the mentoring opportunity that will be waiting when they return in the fall.

Sample CAMP implementation time line

The time line below provides a sample of the tasks that take place throughout the first year (plus) of the program.

Month	Tasks and Program Activities
May	<ul><li>Form an advisory committee</li><li>Assess the need for the program</li><li>Get buy-in from leadership at participating schools</li><li>Develop staffing plan</li><li>Initiate outreach to community partners</li></ul>
June	<ul><li>Identify a Program Coordinator</li><li>Develop program policies and procedures</li><li>Identify potential school liaisons</li><li>Inform faculty about the program, explain the goals of the program and the roles faculty will play</li><li>Get signed MOUs from participating schools/partners</li><li>Arrange for match-meeting space and transportation of participants</li></ul>
July	<ul><li>Review the *CAMP Connectedness Curriculum*</li><li>Select connectedness domains (see Chapter 8) and set the activity calendar for the year</li><li>Review the *CAMP Mentor Training Guide* and prepare initial orientation and training for mentors</li><li>Prepare background information and permission forms for parents of both mentors and mentees</li><li>Develop mentor recruitment materials and talking points</li></ul>
August	<ul><li>Meet with school liaisons and other school staff to discuss roles and responsibilities</li><li>Review program policies and procedures with school leadership and the advisory committee</li><li>Announce the program to potential participants and their parents as the school year begins</li><li>Work with teachers to identify potential Lead Mentors in the school</li></ul>
September	<ul><li>Recruit potential mentors and mentees</li><li>Secure parent permission for participation</li><li>Interview mentors and send notices of acceptance into the program</li><li>Hold initial mentor orientation</li><li>Conduct prematch mentor training</li><li>Prepare mentees for their match</li><li>Explain and distribute the *Hemingway Measure* and other evaluation-related surveys</li><li>Train Lead Mentors</li></ul>
October	<ul><li>Initiate Meet-and-Greet activities (where mentors and mentees first meet each other)</li><li>Hold first SuperSaturday kick-off event</li><li>Finalize one-to-one mentoring matches</li><li>Coordinate *CAMP Connectedness Curriculum* activities for matches to do weekly after school</li></ul>

November	• Check in with Lead Mentors to see how matches are doing and revise curriculum as needed
	• Continue afterschool meetings
	• Conduct first in series of ongoing training for mentors
December	• Hold second SuperSaturday event
	• Continue afterschool meetings
	• Check in with advisory committee on program progress
January	• Give mentors and mentees the match-quality survey to identify matches that may be struggling
	• Conduct the second ongoing training for mentors
February	• Hold the third SuperSaturday event
	• Continue afterschool meetings
March	• Continue afterschool meetings
	• Check in with Lead Mentors to see how matches are doing and revise curriculum as needed
	• Conduct the third ongoing training for mentors
April	• Hold the fourth SuperSaturday event
	• Continue afterschool meetings
May	• Begin to prepare matches for the end of the year
	• Conduct the fourth ongoing training for mentors
	• Prepare end-of-year surveys for parents, teachers, mentors, and other stakeholders
June	• Administer the second *Hemingway Measure* and any other pre/post instruments
	• Gather all parent, teacher, and mentor surveys
	• Hold final meeting with Lead Mentors to assess the year and recommend changes for next year
	• Engage matches in the Match Termination Ritual
	• Hold the final SuperSaturday event—participant recognition and celebration
	• Conduct the end-of-year advisory committee meeting
July	• Review participant feedback and evaluation results
	• Make needed changes to program policies or procedures
August	• Reconvene the advisory committee
	• Meet with school liaisons and other school staff to discuss roles and responsibilities
	• Announce the program to mentors and the parents of mentees as the school year begins
	• Rematch any matches that are continuing for a second year

Key questions for program implementation

There are many details that go into planning and launching a new CAMP at your school. The following self-assessment questions, based on the core CAMP components presented in the previous chapter, can help you work through the many decisions to be made and keep track of your progress. *Keep in mind that information found in the remaining chapters of this manual will help answer many of these questions.*

1. Program infrastructure and start-up

- Have we secured buy-in from the leadership at potential participating schools? How has that buy-in been expressed?

- Are the participating schools a good fit for CAMP in terms of:
  - Geographic proximity
  - Physical space available
  - Resources for the program
  - Student needs and compatibility with each other
  - Level of commitment to the program

- Are there community partners (such as mentoring nonprofits) that could help implement CAMP? Have we done any outreach to these groups?

- Have we secured formal MOUs with all participating schools and partner organizations?

- Do the MOUs address:
  - Staff responsibilities
  - Provision of resources or space
  - Time lines
  - Points of contact

- Who should serve on our advisory committee? Who are our critical stakeholders?

- Have we identified other programs at the schools (such as a traditional afterschool program) that might compete with CAMP for resources or space?

- How will mentors get to the mentees' school? Is it walkable or do we need to arrange for transportation? What transportation options will our mentors and Lead Mentors have?

- What is our available budget? Does it cover:
  - The Program Coordinator position and other core staffing
  - The cost of space or supplies for meeting activities
  - Transportation for participants
  - Supplemental pay for teachers or other school staff that assist the program
  - Costs associated with SuperSaturday events and field trips
  - Food, drinks, and other snacks
  - Administrative costs
  - Funds for program evaluation
  - Printing of materials

- Have we started developing the formal policies and procedures that will govern program operations? Will the Program Coordinator be responsible for this task? If so, what program or school leadership will need to approve these policies?

2. The CAMP theory and philosophy

- Is there agreement within the advisory committee about the goals and purpose of the program? What outcomes do we want for our mentors and mentees? Do those outcomes align with CAMP's traditional results?

- Why do we think a developmental program such as CAMP can support our students? Have we done a formal assessment of student needs or a gap analysis of other available services?

- Have there been previous efforts to address these needs at the participating schools? How well did they work?

- How well do we understand core CAMP concepts, such as perspective taking, connectedness, and the importance of the Termination Ritual? Do we "get" CAMP? If not, how can we deepen our understanding?

3. Program staffing

- What qualities and qualifications do we want in our Program Coordinator?

- When do we want the coordinator position filled?

- Are there existing teachers, counselors, or other staff who could serve as the Program Coordinator?

- Do we have office space for the Program Coordinator? Is there space to meet with Lead Mentors to work on the curriculum and discuss progress?

- Have we identified school liaisons at each of the participating schools? What qualities should our liaisons have? Do they have the time to devote to CAMP and do they need additional compensation for taking on the CAMP liaison role?

- Are the teachers at each school on board with the program? What information do we need to provide to generate excitement?

- What role will teachers play in the program during the course of the year? Will they identify potential participants? Are there *CAMP Connectedness Curriculum* activities that require their participation? How else can they support CAMP?

- What role will the school counselors play in CAMP? How can they help with identifying participants, delivering mentor training, or working with parents?

- What administrative supports will our CAMP need? Do we have available administrative support? What will administrative staff need to know about the program?

4. Program participants

- What qualities are we looking for in our mentors? Our Lead Mentors? What traits will help them be successful?

- How will we screen our mentors? What minimum criteria for participation should they be able to meet?

- What recruitment messages might resonate with our students? What will they have questions or concerns about? What will excite them?

- Should we offer mentors or Lead Mentors class or graduation credit as part of their CAMP experience? Can this be integrated into an existing class? Would that help or hinder the development of CAMP?

- How will mentees be identified or selected for participation?

- How will we secure parent permission for mentees, mentors, and Lead Mentors? How should we describe the program to parents? What questions will they have? How will we reach out to parents?

- How will we track program participants? Can we modify and use an existing school database or do we need to create a program-specific tracking tool?

5. Meetings and activities

- How will we make mentor-mentee matches? Will we use the Meet-and-Greet activity or are there other ideas we want to try?

- Will we have a formal matching ceremony?

- Are there any logistical issues with the weekly afterschool meetings?

- Where will matches primarily meet at the host/mentees' school?

- Will matches need access to additional parts of the campus (such as the library or gym)?

- Who will assist the school liaison and Lead Mentors in supervising matches? Do other staff members need to be involved?

- Are there any scheduling conflicts or timing issues we anticipate in providing the program during the course of the year? Have we accounted for holiday and spring breaks in the schedule and sequence of the curriculum?

- What supplies do we need to have on hand when matches meet? Is there storage space for these materials when CAMP is not meeting?

- What will we do when a mentor or mentee cannot meet in a given week? Will we have mentors or mentees double up? Will they pair with a Lead Mentor for the day?

- Where will SuperSaturdays be held? Are there any challenges or unique opportunities provided by the venue we have chosen?

- What curriculum activities do we want to offer during SuperSaturdays?

- What types of fun field trips or group events would be a hit on SuperSaturdays?

- What kind of participation can we expect and how can we make it engaging, especially for parents?

- Are we going to provide the Summer Program aspect of CAMP? Do we have the resources to do it? How will it enhance the regular program?

6. Participant training and supervision

- In what ways do we need to customize or supplement the *CAMP Mentor Training Guide* materials? How can we make the training more applicable to our particular students?

- When and where will we hold our mentor trainings? Who will conduct them?

- What role will Lead Mentors play in training mentors? Can they deliver part of the training or otherwise share their wisdom with the mentors?

- Will the sequence in which we are implementing the *CAMP Connectedness Curriculum* activities influence when we do certain trainings during the course of the year?

- What questions might our mentors have, especially early in the year?

- What issues might come up for matches during the year?

- How will we support matches that are struggling? What kinds of support will the Lead Mentors provide and when might the Program Coordinator get directly involved?

- Under what circumstances will we rematch a mentor or mentee?

- How will mentors report their activities during the year? Is there a specific form or tracking system we want to use? Who will be responsible for collecting and analyzing this information?

- How will we recognize and celebrate our matches?

- How will we ensure that the Termination Ritual is a fun, positive, and appropriate experience for our students?

- If matches want to continue the following school year, how can we keep them in contact during the summer months?

- How will we encourage mentors to move on to the Lead Mentor role? What incentives can we offer?

7. CAMP Connectedness Curriculum

- What elements of the *CAMP Connectedness Curriculum* align with our schools' goals and objectives? Do we need to create additional activities to supplement or modify the curriculum?

- Which curriculum modules will we do during the year? What sequence makes the most sense?

- What other youth development or group mentoring curricula could we draw from for additional activities?

- What process will the Program Coordinator use to solicit feedback about the curriculum from participants? How will the coordinator work with the Lead Mentors to make needed changes?

- Has the advisory committee reviewed and approved the curriculum? Do any other school personnel need to sign off on the curriculum or specific activities?

8. Program evaluation

- Have we read the Hemingway scale and the evaluation chapter in this guide? What questions do we have about it? Do we feel confident about administering this instrument?

- Should we work with an external evaluator? Why or why not?

- If we decide to work with an external evaluator, where can we find one? Can the school district provide or recommend one? Could a community partner bring this expertise to the table?

- In addition to connectedness, what else do we want to measure in our mentors and mentees? Do these other measures align with the goals and philosophy of CAMP?

- Have we developed a logic model for the program?

- Are there questions that our funders will want answered? Are we collecting data that will give them the information they need?

- How will we disseminate our evaluation findings? Who are the critical stakeholders that will need to be informed?

CHAPTER 3. STAFF ROLES AND RESPONSIBILITIES

There are many individuals who must work together to make CAMP a success in a school or other youth services setting. This chapter clarifies the roles and responsibilities of the CAMP staff: the Program Coordinator, liaisons, teachers, and other professionals who manage the program and facilitate the participant experience. Chapter 4 addresses the role that students and their parents play in a typical program.

The CAMP Program Coordinator

The Program Coordinator is primarily responsible for the start-up and ongoing management of a program. He or she manages the relationships with participating schools and stakeholders; recruits and trains students in the program; works with participants to implement the *CAMP Connectedness Curriculum*; and manages the overall program evaluation and improvement over time.

Beyond these tasks, the Program Coordinator must be the "face" of the program. He or she must engage all participants and nurture enthusiasm for what the program is trying to accomplish. Most mentoring programs succeed because of the strong leadership of a key individual, which is why we recommend that the Program Coordinator be at least a .5 FTE position.

Program Coordinator duties. While the Program Coordinator will likely have a hand in all aspects of program implementation, there are several duties that are critical to the success of any CAMP effort:

Securing buy-in from the participating schools. As discussed in the previous chapter, this initial buy-in is essential so that the program has the support of the entire school community. But even if there is strong initial support for the program, school-based interventions such as CAMP often suffer from "turf wars," conflicts over resources, and misunderstandings as the details of the program are sorted out. The Program Coordinator needs to work with stakeholders to maintain the initial enthusiasm, navigate any challenges, and incorporate feedback about the program into subsequent program changes. First and foremost, the Program Coordinator must nurture a culture where CAMP can thrive.

Developing program materials. This manual, along with the *CAMP Connectedness Curriculum* and *Mentor Training Guide,* provides coordinators with templates for developing a wide range of program handouts, forms, and worksheets. However, all materials should be customized with information specific to your program and should incorporate language that speaks to your students, parents, teachers, and school staff. Program Coordinators must also develop the program's policies and procedures, capturing these in a formal policy manual that will guide the decision making and day-to-day operations of the program. Don't discount the importance of these print (or electronic) materials in implementing CAMP—they are the backbone of any solid mentoring program and provide continuity if the Program Coordinator leaves the program.

Managing the advisory committee. While there is a lot on the coordinator's plate, he or she is not in this alone. The Program Coordinator should convene the advisory committee on a regular basis and use members' skills to help with key tasks throughout the year.

Recruiting and managing CAMP participants. The CAMP coordinator must also recruit mentors and mentees for the program early in the program cycle. The Program Coordinator then oversees participant screening, training, matching, support, supervision, recognition, and closure activities. Some support is provided by Lead Mentors, teachers, and others, but the coordinator ensures that all goes according to plan.

Reaching out to parents and families. One of the key aspects of CAMP is the involvement of parents and families at various points throughout the year, such as during SuperSaturdays. Early in the year, the Program Coordinator should talk with parents of mentors and mentees about what the program can do for their child, why they might want to get involved (or why their child has been referred), and the requirements of participation. During the course of the year, the Program Coordinator should encourage attendance at the SuperSaturday events and work to make parents feel like an integral part of the program.

Adapting the CAMP Connectedness Curriculum. When the program starts up, the Program Coordinator will need to work with the advisory committee to select and sequence activities from the CAMP Connectedness Curriculum or identify other sources of activities that would be appropriate for the program. Over time, the coordinator will work with Lead Mentors to revise the curriculum, removing activities that were not a "hit" and finding new ones that will resonate with participating students.

Overseeing program evaluation and using feedback to make improvements. The Program Coordinator is responsible for administering the Hemingway scale and any other evaluation instruments. Even if your program is working with an external evaluator, the coordinator will be the person responsible for gathering all of the surveys, scheduling focus groups, and sharing evaluation results with key program stakeholders.

Helping with program sustainability. The school-based nature of CAMP means that program funding will be closely tied to school budgets and other financial decisions that are out of the Program Coordinator's control. But, depending on your program's circumstances, the Program Coordinator might take the lead in working with district administration to secure funds, approaching foundations or other private funding sources, and/or writing grant proposals. In some instances, individual giving campaigns or fund-raising events might be in order. However, it's important not to let the search for ongoing funds detract from the maintenance of the program itself. Remember that in CAMP—as with all quality mentoring programs—the needs of the youth always come first.

Note that there is one task that does not appear on this list of Program Coordinator duties: direct work with the mentors and mentees during their match meeting time. Although it is not always possible, we recommend that Program Coordinators give school liaisons and Lead Mentors as much responsibility as possible for working directly with the mentors and mentees. When coordinators get too involved in providing direct service, it leaves less time to attend to big-picture tasks such as building partnerships or developing program materials. It also makes it harder for coordinators to address absent mentors, inadequate school facilities, transportation issues, and other problems as they arise. Putting Lead Mentors or liaisons in charge of leading the curriculum activities frees the coordinator to keep other aspects of the program running smoothly.

This does not mean that the coordinator is *never* around during match activities. Program Coordinators still need to be able to see the curriculum in action, get a sense of how it is going, and provide guidance to mentors and Lead Mentors as they work through activities. Remember, though, that while the coordinators are the face of the program, asking them to be involved in everything may stretch them too thin and leave some big issues untended.

Program Coordinator skills and qualifications. In order to handle the many tasks described above, Program Coordinators will need to bring a diverse skill set to their program. When identifying a potential coordinator, look for an individual who has:

Experience working in a youth development (preferably mentoring) environment. Teachers and counselors often make good Program Coordinators, provided they have the available time. However, even if your potential candidate has experience working in schools, it may not mean that he or she has a strong youth development background or the ability to relate well to young people. Your coordinator should have a proven track record of working with young people in a developmental context and must understand that CAMP is not an academic or remedial program, but rather a program dedicated to personal development and growth.

Experience developing and delivering a curriculum to students. Closely tied to a background in youth development is prior experience using a curriculum with groups of students. The Program Coordinator must be able to effectively schedule and sequence activities from the *CAMP Connectedness Curriculum* (or other sources), refine activities as needed, and develop new activities that fit the culture and focus of CAMP.

Strong oral and written communication skills. Being a CAMP Program Coordinator is all about personal contact: Advisory committee members, principals and administrators, teachers, counselors, parents, and students all rely on the coordinator to provide information and address problems as they arise. This means that the Program Coordinator will need to be comfortable speaking to groups of stakeholders, delivering training, and talking to parents about their child's participation. Since CAMP uses many handouts, fliers, worksheets, permission slips, and other forms, strong writing skills are also a must.

Leadership skills. In addition to having strong communication skills, CAMP coordinators need to be effective leaders. They must be comfortable serving in a leadership role and able to display confidence and competence. They must be able to handle conflict effectively and work with a diverse set of individuals. And most important, they must be able to nurture the leadership abilities of the Lead Mentors and mentors, serving as a role model of what effective leadership looks like and teaching others how to overcome barriers and make good decisions. Be sure to search for candidates who have previous experience in leadership roles.

Compliance with school or district policies. If the coordinator is going to be a school or district employee, he or she must be able to pass background checks and other screening processes. If the coordinator is a contractor, make sure that the individual is eligible to serve in that position and that your program is diligent in following school or district contractor policies.

Available time. This last qualification is perhaps the most critical. As recommended earlier in this manual, the CAMP Program Coordinator should be *at least* a half-time (.5 FTE) position. Programs that give the CAMP coordinator too few hours run the risk of either lowering the quality of the program or burning out the coordinator as he or she tries to fit in CAMP duties around other work tasks. CAMP is not a program that can be implemented in a staff member's spare time, so be sure to find the funds and hours needed to position your Program Coordinator for success.

A sample job description for the CAMP Program Coordinator appears in Appendix B. Modify this document to make the role appropriate for your site.

School liaisons

School liaisons are responsible for arranging transportation to and from the participating schools and overseeing the matches during the weekly meetings. They serve as the point of contact at each school and work to make sure that CAMP has the necessary space, resources, and supplies. They also help manage activities at the SuperSaturday events.

Liaisons are typically teachers, teacher aides, counselors, or afterschool program staff members who stay after the regular school day to help monitor the program. Ideally, there would be two liaisons present for each afterschool meeting: one accompanying the high school mentors and the other representing the host elementary school. The liaisons work together (and with Lead Mentors) to introduce curricular activities, supervise matches while they meet, and keep the group on schedule.

Try to choose liaisons with experience managing a classroom or group youth work environment. CAMP meetings can be noisy, active environments, and it takes skill to be able to manage a group with such diverse ages. Make sure that your liaisons relate well to students and understand how to structure the time without turning the CAMP into a typical classroom experience.

If using teachers or other school staff in this role you may want to provide a stipend or supplemental pay for the extra time they spend serving the program. Liaisons who are not satisfied with their role (or compensation) can obviously impact the effectiveness of a program.

Teachers and other school staff

Teachers can play a variety of roles in the CAMP framework. How they support your particular CAMP will be determined by the time and resources available, but generally, teachers at CAMP schools help by:

Referring students to the program. Teachers are instrumental in identifying younger students who could benefit from having a mentor, recruiting the high school mentors, and identifying students with the leadership skills to serve as Lead Mentors.

Participating in *CAMP Connectedness Curriculum* activities. For example, one activity asks the mentor-mentee pair to interview a teacher about his or her life and job, and report back to the group. Involving teachers in the curriculum is one of the main ways CAMP increases connectedness to school.

Assisting with mentor training, mentee orientation, and parent involvement. Teachers have many skills in working with youth and parents that could be brought to your outreach and training efforts.

Helping with SuperSaturday activities. Teachers can facilitate or monitor activities and serve as chaperones on field trips. Their presence at SuperSaturdays really conveys to parents that the whole school is behind CAMP.

Identifying new curricular activities. Teachers have access to activities and lesson plans that could be a good fit for CAMP. Meet with them often to see if they have suggestions or resources that could improve your match activities.

Other school staff can play a role as well:

Librarians can make their space available for match meetings or work with mentors to identify books or materials that can enhance *CAMP Connectedness Curriculum* activities (especially for the connectedness to reading module).

Counselors can be valuable in identifying potential participants, delivering mentor training, serving as liaisons, or helping matches that are having difficulties work through any issues.

Principals and administrators can support the program by making sure appropriate resources and space are available (and negotiating any turf wars). They can also get parents excited about the program, make sure teachers and other staff are filling their CAMP roles, serve on the advisory committee, participate in SuperSaturday events, and secure new partnerships and ongoing funding.

Secretaries and front office staff can help mentors and Lead Mentors feel comfortable coming to the mentees' campus and can troubleshoot any logistical problems such as building access or transportation issues. They can also be instrumental in contacting parents and participating students, especially when mentors or mentees will miss meetings.

In addition to the Program Coordinator, liaisons, and other staff, there may be community members and institutions that can play a role in your CAMP—staff at nonprofit partners and local businesses, parent volunteers, and so forth. This will help in building buy-in for the program and may ultimately contribute to sustainability.

CHAPTER 4. PROGRAM PARTICIPANTS

One of the best attributes of the CAMP model is that it benefits many different participants. While most mentoring programs (even peer-led ones) are solely focused on the development of the *mentee,* CAMP has demonstrated positive outcomes for three levels of youth participants: mentees, mentors, and Lead Mentors. Additionally, by involving parents, CAMP can also have a positive impact on the relationships within families.

However, these positive outcomes depend on getting the right mix of youth and families involved in the program. Each student (and his or her parent) has a role to play in making CAMP a success. This chapter reviews the roles and responsibilities of mentors, Lead Mentors, mentees, and parents. It also provides tips for identifying and recruiting participants who will be a good fit for CAMP. Subsequent chapters further explain participants' training, activities, and support.

Mentors

Mentors in the CAMP model are typically high school sophomores and juniors. Occasionally seniors serve as mentors, but more frequently they fulfill the role of Lead Mentor. This is especially true if they have already been a mentor in the program. Choosing sophomores as mentors increases the likelihood of matches lasting more than one year, which is something seniors inherently can't provide.

CAMP mentors work directly with the younger mentees, and this relationship is the core intervention of the CAMP model. The *CAMP Connectedness Curriculum* is designed so that the mentor will benefit from the program activities as much as the mentee. By meeting with their mentee and providing that critical praise, empathy, and attention, mentors themselves grow developmentally in important ways. The weekly meetings and the structure of the overall CAMP year allow mentors to practice new skills, solve problems, and model positive behaviors. Thus, the main role of mentors is to attend the match meetings consistently and participate in the activities.

Mentor responsibilities:

- Attend the weekly meetings and SuperSaturday events throughout the year
- Inform the Program Coordinator if unable to make a match meeting
- Attend all orientations and trainings (including ongoing training)
- Follow all program guidelines on mentor behavior (staying on task, being respectful, modeling positive behaviors, focusing on the mentee, etc.)
- Complete all evaluation surveys and other program paperwork
- Report on match activities and provide other feedback as required

Mentor skills and qualifications. Because mentors work directly with mentees, they must possess or develop several characteristics that will help them in this role. Important traits for CAMP mentors include strong interpersonal skills, strength of character, and the ability to understand others' perspectives in order to help them achieve their goals. (See the sidebar for additional characteristics to look for in CAMP mentors.)

There is a common myth that the best peer mentors are students who are already having tremendous personal success in school—in other words, the "straight A" students. In reality, while these students may have many admirable traits that could help them as mentors, they also tend to have numerous commitments that can get in the way. It will do more harm than good if the high-achieving mentors miss meetings because of other obligations.

Another consideration is that by using mentors who are already high-quality students with little need for focused development, you are essentially eliminating half of the potential impact of CAMP. If you choose mentors who have some needs of their own, they can benefit from the mentoring experience as much as the mentees do.

There are several factors to consider when deciding who should serve as a mentor:

Age and year in school. There should be an age difference of at least two years and/or two grades between the CAMP mentor and mentee. This gap is considered an important factor in maintaining boundaries in the relationship. There is also some evidence that high school mentors are more effective than middle-schoolers (if your program is considering using them), as they may be developmentally more prepared to use good judgment, maintain boundaries, and be a "wise and trusted friend" (Karcher, 2007).

Availability. Mentors need to be available to participate in weekly match meetings, initial and ongoing training, and other CAMP activities. While no youth is likely to be available for *every* activity, it is important to choose students who are not overcommitted. This helps ensure that they will follow through with their responsibilities to the program. Because of the cross-campus nature of CAMP, be sure to ask potential mentors about any transportation issues that may complicate their involvement.

Overall length of commitment. Another important consideration is overall match duration, both in terms of a single school year and over multiple years. Do not accept mentors who know in the fall that they will not be enrolled in the school for the full year. Also consider how important multiyear matches are to your goals. Programs generally strive to involve students for many years, as this leads to even stronger relationships and enhanced outcomes.

Social interest and positive attitudes toward youth. Prospective mentors typically have a high level of "social interest." This is generally indicated by a positive outlook, personal optimism, a genuine desire to be helpful to others, and expressions of empathy. Mentors should also exhibit positive attitudes toward mentees and youth in general, in order to forge strong relationships. CAMP uses two scales to help determine the social interest and attitudes of prospective mentors. Candidates who score a 10 or above on the *Social Interest Scale* (Crandall, 1991, see Appendix C) are generally seen as good mentor material (Karcher & Lindwall, 2003). Research also suggests that individuals who score a 3.5 or above on the *Mentor Attitudes Toward Youth* scale (see Appendix C) will likely be a good fit for the peer mentoring experience (Karcher, Davidson, Rhodes, & Herrera, 2010).

Strong connectedness. Potential mentors also complete the *Hemingway Measure of Adolescent Connectedness* (Karcher & Sass, 2010), which may prove instructive in selecting a pool of mentors with diverse backgrounds, attributes, and experiences. Mentors who already have strong

Characteristics of Effective Peer (CAMP) Mentors

- Demonstrate interpersonal competence, integrity, and stability
- Are supportive, flexible, patient, other-centered, and tolerant
- Can commit to programs, people, and projects even when there are other demands in their lives
- Are skilled in friendship development and maintenance
- Are interested in sharing information and empowering others to develop skills and talents
- Possess good communication, listening, and problem-solving skills
- Are interested in working with youth
- Aspire to a career in the helping professions
- Can have fun with others in both structured and unstructured settings

connectedness may be in a position to help others develop this attribute. You may choose not to use this measure as a factor in mentor selection. However, mentors will still complete this assessment prior to working with their mentees since discussing the mentee's connectedness profile is one of the early CAMP Connectedness Curriculum activities. The first training mentors receive is on connectedness, so this scale should be completed before that initial training.

Grades and school performance/behavior. As noted previously, there is no evidence that honors students make better mentors than those with average grades. Consistent attendance, passing grades, and participation in school activities indicate stability in a prospective mentor. Mentors who are consistently present will forge stronger relationships with their mentees, so value reliability more than good grades when selecting mentor candidates. However, keep in mind that positive school performance can be an indicator of positive connections to school and community, which are attitudes the program aims to foster in mentees.

Special skills. Although most programs do not require mentors to have special skills, there may be situations in which a certain skill could be beneficial, including the ability to speak a second language, strength in a particular subject area (e.g., math or science), or experience with a particular population of children (e.g., those with physical disabilities). Special skills will be particularly helpful if your CAMP targets a specific subgroup of students, such as adolescent immigrants or children whose second language is English.

See Appendix B for a mentor "job description" template that further details roles, responsibilities, and qualifications for CAMP mentors.

Recruiting mentors

How you recruit mentors will depend on the size and scope of your program. We usually encourage new programs to start small, with 10–15 matches, so that you can work out the kinks and then scale up the program once it is ready. If you are recruiting a small batch of mentors, recruitment generally can be handled by working with counselors, teachers, and other school staff to identify students who might be a good fit.

If your program is going to serve a larger number of matches, or operate at multiple schools within the district, a more generalized recruitment campaign is in order. Teachers and other staff should still identify prospective mentors to directly approach, but you may also want to consider other methods, including:

Provide CAMP information at parent orientation events (especially at the beginning of the year). The Program Coordinator should develop a brief presentation for parents emphasizing the benefits to students and how parents can play a role in the connectedness outcomes CAMP strives for. If opportunities to talk to parents are limited, teachers can cover this information during initial parent-teacher conferences.

Develop CAMP brochures, posters, and other materials. Work with students in the school's art program to develop fun and eye-catching recruitment materials. Ask students for their input in what kinds of messages might appeal to their peers. If possible, include some of these materials in school mailings to parents, especially at the beginning of the year.

Encourage teachers to promote the program in class. Ask the school liaisons to provide teachers with information about the program and arrange for brief presentations at the beginning of the year.

Some ambitious programs enlist their mentors through special classes on service-learning, human development, psychology, or related academic topics. In these situations, mentors' time spent in training and with the mentee count as class activities, supplemented by other classroom content and exams. This approach can make multiyear matches less likely. But, if you can connect the program to student course credit or a formal class, this can be an effective way of ensuring a steady pool of mentors each year.

Mentor orientation and application

Once you have identified prospective mentors, the next step is to conduct an orientation session that motivates your new recruits and helps them feel like they have a chance to be part of something special at the school.

Most CAMPs provide an afterschool orientation that lasts about half an hour, covering:

- Purpose and goals of the program, both for mentees and mentors
- General eligibility to participate in the program (age, school class, etc.)
- Amount of time commitment expected
- What participation in the program looks like (afterschool activities, SuperSaturdays)
- Introduction to the Program Coordinator and school liaisons
- Benefits of participating (such as the opportunity to be involved in an extracurricular activity, the chance to fulfill a graduation service requirement, and the possibility of meeting new friends)
- Next steps for formally applying to the program

If prospective mentors are still interested after the orientation, you should provide them with an application packet that includes:

- An application (see Appendix B)
- An information sheet that details program goals, expectations, schedules, and rules
- Ideally, a letter of support from the school principal
- Contact information for the Program Coordinator
- A permission form for parents to sign
- An explanation of the enrollment process once the application is returned

If you are using the *Social Interest Scale* and the *Mentors Attitudes Toward Youth* scale as tools to determine who to accept into the program, include this in the application packet as well.

Determining if students are a good fit as mentors

Unlike adult-youth mentoring programs, where prospective mentors go through a variety of rigorous screening procedures to ensure that they can safely work with young people, peer mentoring programs employ different techniques to identify and screen potential mentors. Most programs use a two-step process:

1. Conduct interviews with mentor applicants. These interviews are designed to assess the mentor's enthusiasm about the opportunity and to see if there will be any barriers to participation. Ask questions such as:

- Why do you want to serve in the program? What do you hope to gain?
- How do you feel about younger students?
- What do you think of school? What would you tell a middle school student about what high school is like?
- What do you like to do for fun out of school? Do you have hobbies or other outside activities?
- Do you have younger siblings in your family? How do you help them?
- Do you think you can make time for the afterschool meetings? How about the SuperSaturday events? Do you or your parents have any transportation concerns?
- What do you like about your friends? What types of things do you do together?

- Have you ever volunteered before? Have you ever participated in something where you helped another person?
- Do you have any questions about the program?

The answers to such questions can help you determine if a student has the temperament, character, and commitment to be a good CAMP mentor. The prospects don't need to give perfect answers, but should demonstrate that their heart is in the right place and that they will be committed to doing the best they can in the program.

2. Check with parents and other personal references. Most CAMPs ask mentors to provide at least one in-school and one out-of-school reference. If the student was initially referred to the program by a teacher or counselor, check in with that individual as well. The referral form in Appendix B solicits information about why the student is being referred. Follow up for additional information about the young person. The more you know about your mentors, the easier it will be to match them with an appropriate mentee.

Be sure to talk with parents of potential mentors. Get their answers to many of the same questions you asked in the mentor interview: Can they picture their son or daughter in a mentoring role? Determine if the program's schedule and the available transportation options will work with the family's weekly schedule. Explain the role that parents will play at SuperSaturdays and other occasional program events. And, make sure you answer any questions parents may have—this initial contact is key in getting parent buy-in for the program.

If there are no red flags during the interview or reference checks, accept the individual into the program. Be clear about the next steps between acceptance and the first mentor-mentee event. Typically, these include:

- Informing parents of the student's acceptance as a mentor and providing a full calendar of events with key dates for the year

- Asking mentors to fill out the *Hemingway Measure*, the *Social Interest Scale,* and the *Mentor Attitudes Toward Youth* scale (if they have not already done so as part of the application)

- Providing the initial prematch training for mentors (see Chapter 7 and the *Mentor Training Guide* for more information)

The most critical aspect of recruiting mentors and preparing them for their match is to make sure that you have answered their (and their parents') questions and calmed their fears at every step of the way. Once you move toward making matches and building these new relationships, you need to be assured that the mentors are excited about the opportunity and confident they can fulfill their obligations. Only move forward with mentors who bring enthusiasm and commitment to the table, so you can build the positive peer culture that will ultimately make the program a success.

Lead Mentors

Lead Mentors play an important role in the program. This position provides seniors and juniors who have mentored in previous years with a developmentally appropriate opportunity to learn and practice new skills. Not all students who served as mentors will move on to Lead Mentor roles—in fact, you should be judicious about who you ask to take on this important assignment. But, becoming a Lead Mentor is a great way for students who were good mentors to use their experience in a leadership role and take on new challenges.

The role of Lead Mentors. There are several tasks that Lead Mentors are responsible for during the year, but their primary responsibility is to lead the *CAMP Connectedness Curriculum* activities during the afterschool meetings and SuperSaturdays. Lead Mentors must be able to keep the mentors on task during meeting times (one of the biggest issues in all peer mentoring programs). Thus, Lead Mentors need to be older students who will command respect from the mentors and who can correct problem behaviors before they undermine the day's goals and activities.

We recommend having two to four Lead Mentors for a typical program (about a 5:1 mentor-to-Lead Mentor ratio) as this allows for easier explanation and supervision of curriculum activities. Lead Mentors work with the school liaisons and Program Coordinator to coordinate the match meetings and provide support to the mentors and mentees as they engage in activities or projects.

In addition to those tasks, the Lead Mentor's responsibilities include:

- Reporting any match problems or program feedback to the Program Coordinator. Lead Mentors are a critical communicator between program participants and the adults in charge of the program.

- Serving as a "temporary" mentor if mentors miss a weekly meeting or SuperSaturday. Lead Mentors can step in and make sure that no mentee is without a partner for that day.

- Assisting with mentor recruitment and the development of program materials, such as posters or handouts.

- Helping to deliver the mentor training. Delivering actual training content builds their skills, and sharing their insights into what it's like to be a mentor in the program can be invaluable to a new batch of mentors.

- Informing mentors about upcoming events and ensuring attendance at the afterschool and SuperSaturday events.

- Helping disseminate and collect program paperwork, such as permission slips for a group outing or surveys.

- Working with the Program Coordinator to improve the curriculum and identify needed adjustments to existing activities. Lead Mentors can also help develop new activities that fit with CAMP goals and philosophies.

Lead Mentors basically make everyone's job in the program easier. They use their experience to guide the younger participants, their leadership skills to help implement day-to-day activities, and their relationships with the students to elicit feedback to help the Program Coordinator make needed changes to the program. While it is possible to run a program without students in this role, it places tremendous pressure on the Program Coordinator or liaisons and removes a vital facilitator of communication between the program staff and participants. We encourage all programs, even new ones, to find responsible students who can fill the Lead Mentor role.

Skills and qualifications of Lead Mentors. When identifying and selecting Lead Mentors, it is important to look for several qualities:

Prior experience as a mentor in CAMP or another peer helping program. Students who have served in a mentoring role (or have been mentored themselves) will have an easier time supporting others in the program.

Strong leadership and communication skills. Consider if prospective Lead Mentors have the respect of other students. Have they assumed leadership positions in other school activities or programs?

A positive attitude about the program and the students it serves. Lead Mentors must demonstrate that they have an affinity for the youth in the program. Remember, mentors who have a positive attitude are much more effective, and the same holds true for Lead Mentors. They must embrace the goals of the program and feel good about supporting the participants.

Available time. Unfortunately, this can be a challenge for Lead Mentors. Often the students who exhibit the desired leadership and communication skills possess those qualities precisely because of their involvement in other programs and extracurricular activities. They may have limited time to devote to CAMP. When selecting Lead Mentors be very honest about the time commitments of the program, especially the match meeting schedule and SuperSaturday events. Lead Mentors can't properly support the program if they frequently miss events.

Additional Lead Mentor qualifications, skills, and responsibilities can be found in the Lead Mentor job description in Appendix B.

Promoting mentors to Lead Mentors. At the end of every program cycle, the Program Coordinator should approach the most successful mentors and ask if they would like to become Lead Mentors. Interviewing students who express a desire to move up to the Lead Mentor role can help you determine if they are up to the challenge. (See the sidebar for sample interview questions.) Do not ask students who struggled as mentors to take on this more advanced job—they are more likely to benefit from the program by staying on as mentors and building their skills in that role.

For mentors who are being considered as Lead Mentors, emphasize that:

- This is a way to help all of the youth in the program, not just one mentee. By being a Lead Mentor, they actually impact many more individuals.

- Serving as a Lead Mentor looks great on a college or job application. The leadership, conflict resolution, collaboration, and public speaking skills they will gain as a Lead Mentor may help them land a job or get into college, but will also improve their chances of finding success throughout their lives.

- They will get plenty of training and support. Serving as a Lead Mentor can be an intimidating idea, so be sure to explain that the Program Coordinator and liaisons will prepare them for the role and provide support throughout the year.

Once you have some students ready to make the leap to Lead Mentor, schedule an orientation toward the end of summer or very early in the school year. Lead Mentors will need to be trained and ready to support the program in time for mentor recruitment and training. The orientation meeting is used to:

- Reiterate their responsibilities and the program expectations, especially the time commitment.

- Provide training in communication skills, problem solving, working with mentors who are misbehaving, leading activities, and other topics (see the *Mentor Training Guide* for additional suggestions).

- Review the time line for the year and the sequence of curriculum activities.

- Review any feedback from the previous year about what worked and what did not; ask if there are changes that need to be made before reaching out to mentors and mentees.

- Introduce the school liaisons, counselors, or other staff who will be working with the Lead Mentors.

Throughout the year, schedule a standing meeting with your Lead Mentors to discuss:

Questions for Potential Lead Mentors

1. Have you ever been in a leadership position? If yes, explain.

2. What would you do in the following situation: You notice that a mentor (who is one of your classmates) is "goofing off" during the program activities?

3. What ideas do you have that might help to keep mentors more engaged throughout the program?

4. Can you commit to the weekly afterschool meetings and SuperSaturday events? Do you have any scheduling conflicts?

5. What do you hope to gain from this experience?

6. Why do you think you would be a good Lead Mentor?

- Upcoming *CAMP Connectedness Curriculum* activities and how they will be presented to the mentors and mentees. Practice introducing each activity and see if the Lead Mentors have any questions about the instructions or their role in making sure the activity goes well.

- Any matches that have been having problems. Lead Mentors may need support from the Program Coordinator or counselor to deal with a match that is struggling or a mentor who is misbehaving. (Remember that Lead Mentors are still youth and may not have the wisdom or experience to deal with all the issues that may come up.)

- Any feedback from program participants. Do the matches seem happy? Bored? What isn't working so far? What changes can be made? Your Lead Mentors may be much more likely to get an honest opinion about the program than the Program Coordinator or liaisons.

Be sure to provide your Lead Mentors with plenty of recognition and praise. Promote their efforts in the school newspaper or program newsletter. Provide them with a small stipend or gifts to let them know their time and effort are appreciated. They are critical to the success of the program, so make sure they can see that their hard work is valued.

Protégés

A protégé is a student who has served at least one year in the developmental mentoring program as a mentee, who is in the seventh or eighth grade, and who desires to receive training to become a mentor. Their duties are to support staff and to practice mentoring a student in the program. Protégés assist when a mentor is absent or struggling. They should possess or have the capacity to develop the qualities of effective mentors, as described above. Eighth-grade mentors may also be included if they are mature, committed, and well supervised. Typically, however, grade 7 and 8 students are utilized as protégés and are seen as mentors-in-training.

Mentees

CAMP mentees are typically students in grades 3–6, although some programs serve middle school–age mentees. Most programs are collaborations between a high school and an elementary school. If you are working with a middle school, remember that there should be at least a two grade/year gap between the mentors and mentees.

Mentees are typically nominated by teachers, counselors, or other school staff members who feel the students could benefit from the mentoring experience. Some CAMPs also ask parents to nominate their children for the program.

Identifying CAMP mentees. Do not assume that CAMP mentees must be youth who are deemed "at risk" or who are facing serious challenges. In fact, one of the worst things a program can do is foster the perception that it is only for "bad kids" or students with severe problems. Programs actually benefit from having a diverse group of mentees (and mentors). The activities are often designed to encourage interaction and cooperation among a variety of peers as a way of building connectedness across typical peer networks.

The ratio of "high-risk" to mainstream students should be 1:5 but can be 1:4 in a well supervised program. That would mean that in an afterschool group of 10–15 mentees (meeting with their mentors, which is 30 kids total) there would only be 2 to 3 kids with demonstrable social, emotional, or behavioral problems, or youth who have a history of misbehavior, misconduct, or peer problems at school. Why? This ratio is critical to avoid the deviancy training process described by Dodge, Dishion, and Lansford (2006). In fact, recent work shows that if you have more balanced groups of high- and low-risk youth—say a 2:5 or 3:5 ratio—the deviancy training processes are accelerated. The peer group acceleration of deviancy is much less likely to happen when the ratio does not allow for a "group" or clique of "high-risk" kids to form in the program.

That being said, most programs do try to involve students who may be shy, struggle to make friends, or face some challenge in school or at home. The reality is that all students are welcome to participate as mentees, provided they can meet the program's schedule and guidelines.

Identify mentees at the beginning of the school year or preferably at the end of the previous school year. Teacher references will be more useful for end-of-spring applicants. In contrast, when possible, give teachers time to get to know or reconnect with the students at the beginning of the year before asking them to make referrals. Be clear about the number of participants you can enroll and set a due date for referrals early in the year. If teachers will be speaking to parents directly about the opportunity, provide them with brochures, permission forms, and other pertinent information.

Once potential mentees have been identified, the Program Coordinator contacts parents to invite them to an orientation that further explains the opportunity. Regardless of how you discuss the student's participation, make sure you get written permission from the parents and let them know that there may be subsequent permissions needed throughout the year for field trips or other program activities. This permission should also cover the administration of the CAMP surveys (such as the *Hemingway* scale) and other data collection needed for program evaluation.

The participation of mentees' parents is quite important in the CAMP model. Involvement in the SuperSaturday events is one of the main ways CAMP fosters connectedness to family. Parents also support their child's participation in other ways, such as ensuring they will attend events or helping with a curriculum project that involves the family. Consequently, it's important to make sure during initial enrollment that the mentee's parents understand:

- The goals of the program
- Why their child was nominated
- The schedule of the afterschool meetings and SuperSaturdays
- Who the mentors are
- How the program is supervised
- How they can support their child's involvement

Answer any questions and inform parents about the next steps in the program (e.g., when the first match meeting takes place). More suggestions about fostering parent buy-in are found later in this chapter.

Once mentees have been fully accepted into the program, have the school liaison provide a brief orientation to the students. Build excitement by asking them what they hope to experience with their new friends. Make sure your orientation to the program covers:

- When they will meet with their mentor
- The types of things they will do together
- Who the coordinator and liaisons are and the role that each will play
- Who the Lead Mentors are
- Where they will meet during afterschool time
- Basic information about the SuperSaturday events
- Simple program rules

Mentees may have many questions or worries about the program. Find ways for them to express their concerns or anxieties, as well as their excitement. Use this initial orientation to set a positive tone for the rest of the year.

Moving toward introducing participants and making matches

Once you have selected your mentors, Lead Mentors, and mentees, the next steps include:

- Conducting the initial training for mentors (see Chapter 7 for additional details).

- Meeting with the Lead Mentors to review the *Connectedness Curriculum* and other planned activities to see if any changes are needed before the beginning of the year.

- Training Lead Mentors on how to supervise matches and offer positive support to program participants.

- Reviewing the schedule of the year with school liaisons to make sure facilities, supplies, and transportation are arranged.

- Introducing mentors and mentees, usually at a special "kick-off" event or initial SuperSaturday. (See Chapter 6 for a description of the Meet-and-Greet activity that most programs use for determining which mentors and mentees will be paired together for the year.)

Parents

As noted previously, parents of both mentors and mentees play a vital role in the success of CAMP. By participating in occasional program activities, such as the SuperSaturdays, they send the message that the program is important to their child and family. The home environment provides the mentor or mentee with a place to practice new skills or mirror positive behaviors they have developed during CAMP. And, at a basic level, parents can be integral to simple program logistics, such as transportation to and from meeting sites or the coordination of off-site events.

Be aware that parents will want to participate at varying levels. Parent involvement can be a challenge for any educational program, and CAMP is no exception. Some parents will be heavily involved while others may only return permission slips. Your program can maximize parent involvement by:

Providing clear information from the very beginning of the year. Make sure they understand the goals of the program, the time commitments for participation, and how they can support the match. There is no such thing as too much communication with parents, especially at the beginning of a program.

Creating a fun and welcoming environment at the four SuperSaturday events held each year. Many parents don't really get a full appreciation for CAMP until they attend the first SuperSaturday event. Seeing all of the other mentors and mentees, along with their families, really brings home the message that CAMP is about creating relationships that support their children. Make sure that the members of your advisory committee are at the initial SuperSaturday event and encourage them to come to as many events as they can. Lead Mentors, teachers, counselors, and other stakeholders can also play a role in making these events fun. We have found that what parents value the most at these events is the opportunity to see their child interact with their mentor or mentee and work together on curriculum activities. Parents participate in the program when they observe the special nature of these relationships.

Checking in frequently during the year. Parents are likely to have many questions, concerns, and suggestions throughout the year, so it's important to establish mechanisms for easy communication (e.g., e-mail, newsletters, a Facebook page). See Chapter 7 for additional information about checking-in with parents as part of the match supervision process.

Involving them in program evaluation. Parents should be surveyed at the end of each CAMP school year (see Chapter 9) to provide valuable information and testimonials that can help tell the story of the program's impact. Share these evaluation results with them. Openly discuss what the program is (and is not) achieving and ask for their suggestions for improvement.

The primary way that parents can support the program is to ensure that their child attends afterschool meetings and SuperSaturday events. However, parents can be supportive in other ways, including:

- Returning permission slips, surveys, and other forms on time
- Volunteering to chaperone program events or off-campus outings
- Participating in curriculum activities that involve the family
- Providing feedback
- Talking to their child about the mentoring experience and providing encouragement
- Attending SuperSaturday events
- Notifying the Program Coordinator when their child will miss a scheduled mentoring meeting
- Serving as a reference to other parents

See Appendix B for permission forms and other templates related to working with CAMP parents, mentors, mentees, and Lead Mentors.

CHAPTER 5. THEORIES BEHIND THE CAMP MODEL

CAMP is a developmental intervention that is based on several well-known theories about youth development and personal growth. It is helpful for Program Coordinators to become well versed in the CAMP theoretical framework in order to keep their program aligned with the CAMP mission and vision.

Why research and theory are important in CAMP

CAMP was developed by Dr. Michael Karcher, a developmental psychologist and a leading expert on youth mentoring, to test whether research and theory on child and adolescent development could be merged with a mentoring model that facilitates personal growth and positive outcomes. There are several reasons why the program was built on cornerstones of research and theory about personal development and change:

It grounds the program in proven ideas. By building on an evidence-based framework, CAMP increases the likelihood of proven positive outcomes. And, by incorporating cutting-edge theory about how youth develop, CAMP encompasses many of the leading ideas about how to best support healthy development.

It structures match activities and the time line of the year. The shape of the mentor-mentee meetings and the program year itself are designed to facilitate personal growth and align with research-based developmental milestones.

It helps the CAMP Program Coordinator improve the program over time. If Program Coordinators have a clear understanding of concepts such as connectedness, perspective taking, and developmental stages they will find it easier to add new curriculum pieces, supplement mentor training, and make other changes to the program without diluting the focus of the mentoring intervention.

It provides measurable goals. One of the best aspects of the CAMP model is that its primary evaluation instrument, the *Hemingway Measure of Adolescent Connectedness,* is in perfect alignment with the goals and activities of the program. Mentoring programs run into problems when their activities do not align with the program goals or the data being collected. CAMP benefits from focusing evaluation on the main thing matches work toward: increased connectedness.

It satisfies the requirements of funders. Many government, foundation, or private funders will only support program models that are "evidence based" or founded on proven principles. CAMP is grounded in more than a century of research into child and adolescent development. It has been evaluated and proven to be an effective model.

Core theories behind CAMP

While Program Coordinators could spend a lifetime learning the nuances of the theory behind CAMP, the following section highlights what we feel are the main principles at work in the CAMP model. Two constructs—connectedness and perspective taking—serve as both the main program outcomes targeted by the mentoring and the basis for the CAMP curriculum and programmatic structure. These two theories reflect core, essential life skills that are the hallmark of social development and interpersonal maturity. Promote these and you are likely to lessen, ameliorate, and prevent many social, behavioral, and academic problems.

Therefore, this chapter defines connectedness and provides illustrations of how this manifests differently across the adolescent social ecology for elementary, middle, and high school students. Using Erikson's developmental theory, it illustrates how connectedness facilitates psychosocial development and explains the primary social development theories we use regarding the promotion of perspective-taking skills and the importance of providing empathy, praise, and attention within a programmatic context of clear, consistent structure.

Adolescent connectedness as the source of self-development

Connectedness defined. Connectedness may be best understood through what one does and cares about. We are connected in terms of what we do in the world and how much we care about a world and the people in it. Cooper (1999) talks about different "worlds" of connection, such that one's connectedness can be to one's self, with others, or in society. The definition of connectedness used in CAMP builds on the tradition of Grotevant and Cooper (1983) and others who have emphasized an ecological model of adolescent connectedness to self, others, and society.

The ecology of adolescent connectedness. CAMP targets four major worlds of connectedness. The four major worlds include connectedness to:

1. School (school and teachers)
2. Family (parents and siblings)
3. Friends (peers/classmates and, indirectly, to romantic partners)
4. Self (both now and in the future)

These elements are depicted in the figure below, guide the connectedness curriculum, and are assessed using the Hemingway scale in the program evaluation described in Chapter 7. These worlds of connectedness also reveal why it is important to involve teachers and parents in the program.

Mentoring programs can address all of these worlds only when the program is nested within larger systems of influence that directly engage the youth in educational, family-inclusive, and future-oriented activities within the context of an ongoing and personally meaningful mentoring relationship.

Connectedness to self, others, and society. Each of three broad connectedness domains—connectedness to self, others, and society—is addressed in the curriculum at different times during the year and in the summer program. Interpersonal connections are the focus of the curriculum in the fall, and then connectedness to self and to reading are the focus of the curriculum in the spring. Finally, connectedness to culture, neighborhood, and the future are all addressed during one or more of the summer programs.

Intrapersonal (self) connectedness. This refers to self-connectedness or a connection to the "self-world." Connectedness to self is reflected in one's self-esteem, cohesiveness of self-in-relationship, and identity. It is one's sense of being liked, skillful, and interesting to others and happy with oneself in the present. This form of connectedness is promoted explicitly in the spring of each year through a set of curricular activities designed to foster self-awareness, self-esteem, and an awareness of one's unique qualities. Self-in-the-future is addressed in the summer program.

Interpersonal (others) connectedness refers to the quality of being actively involved in meaningful relationships with others. Connectedness to others is captured by the quality and degree of one's independence, involvement with others, and appreciation for or interest in others. These forms of

**Figure 1.
Connectedness to
Self, Others, and
Society**

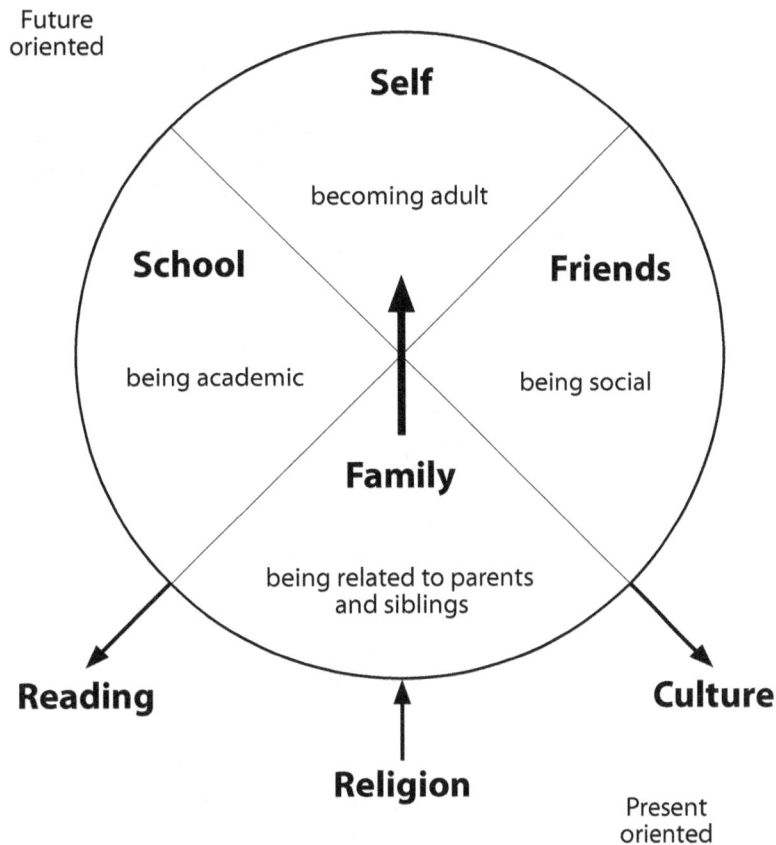

connectedness are targeted explicitly in the fall of each year through curricular activities designed to foster connectedness to teachers, friends, and peers (classmates). Connectedness to parents, another form of interpersonal connectedness, is fostered primarily through the SuperSaturday events where the children, their mentors, and their parents interact.

Environmental (society) connectedness reflects one's involvement in and concern for people and places in the larger society—to broader (often abstract and intangible) worlds (e.g., culture). Because connectedness is believed to be a reciprocation of social support received in these contexts (Karcher, Holcomb, & Zambrano, 2008), we view these contextual worlds of connectedness as best targeted at the end of the school year once youth have experienced a sense of safety and community within the program. Environmental connectedness—connectedness to society—is important because it likely is a primary source of one's degree of social interest or altruistic engagement in the world. This includes connectedness to other cultures (and to peers from different cultures), connectedness to neighborhood, school, and religion, as well as connectedness to the world of reading.

Connectedness promotion efforts in CAMP (Erikson's developmental model)

The developmental aspects of connectedness must be considered in planning the program. A world that is "connecting" for an individual at age nine, such as a neighborhood with its playground, will not necessarily be as connecting at age sixteen, at least not for the same reasons or in the same ways. While there are worlds of connectedness that transcend developmental changes, such as having a supportive family, many worlds of connectedness vary in their importance between childhood and adolescence (Garmezy, 1981).

Erik Erikson (1950) suggested that at different times in life there are specific tasks with which each individual is presented. These tasks are structured by society and also are guided by social, emotional, and cognitive developments that lead youth of different ages to prioritize different elements of a given world of connection. For instance, the elementary student may work toward task mastery or role experimentation in school, whereas the sixteen-year-old may see school as a place to expand social relations and achieve a balance between feelings of intimacy and identity. This illustrates how two different manifestations of connectedness occur in the same world (i.e., school) but at different points in development, such that connectedness to school, for instance, may be strengthened differently for mentors and mentees at the time, while together, but as a result of different roles for each.

Self-developments

At each stage of psychosocial development, there are the self-developments "under construction." These self-developments are shaped by the history of connectedness experienced to that date. What we do, what we value, the skills we develop—all of these are shaped by the people with whom we felt connected and spent time in past relationships. Those with positive experiences and connections with teachers seek out mastery of academic skills and academic identities; whereas those lacking supportive adults in the home and school often feel compelled to develop skills that will garner them esteem and worth from their peers, friends, and others in their neighborhood.

In this way, preadolescent connectedness in elementary school contributes to both the self-developments in middle school and also adolescent connectedness in high school (Karcher & Benne, 2008). This is what the model in Figure 2 is meant to convey. Of course, there are no periods when one is only focusing on connectedness or only focusing on self-developments. These occur in tandem, but because we are complex individuals, we can be heavily focused on relationships in particular contexts (e.g., home, neighborhood, school) and at other times and in other contexts be more focused on skill development.

Revisiting Erikson's Stages

Many of us have heard of the Eriksons' stages of psychosocial development, but they bear repeating just to be sure. In order to avoid any mistranslation, I'll present the four stages of concern to us, and do so in the Eriksons' own words when possible. A second point these quotes convey is that understanding only these self-developments (industry and identity) is insufficient to fully grasp the power and importance of mentoring. Adolescent connectedness serves as the glue in between each of these developmental stages or strengths.

The Industry stage is where sense of competence is the strength to be developed. This is not necessarily or only academic but also where the child starts to learn and navigate the social world of school as practice and preparation for the world of work in the future. Mentors must keep in mind that those who do not find that their homes and schools afford opportunities for the experience of industry will experience a tension or pull in another direction when approaching the task of identity formation. This "counter pull is sense of inferiority or inadequacy" (Erikson, 1988, p. 92). For our students, we must do all we can in Elementary and Middle School to ensure that they have opportunities to master the stage of industry both by providing an arena to demonstrate competence, but also by providing a relationship context wherein those strengths can be mirrored back to the youth.

Identify formation is the next stage, and it is most relevant to our mentors personally because it is the task before them. The nature of their readiness to initiate this task depends on the outcome of the prior stages. Identity as "a sense of fidelity to oneself and to one's own values, to coworkers, associates, and ideologies is the strength to be fostered. For this to be even temporarily experienced, a unique sense of personal identity must emerge" (Erikson, 1988, pp. 95–96). Training in relational skills development and feedback provided to mentors by program staff have the potential to directly influence the development of the mentor's emergent identity, and thereby shape the mentors'

Figure 2. The Relationship Between Connectedness, Self-Development, and in CAMP Roles

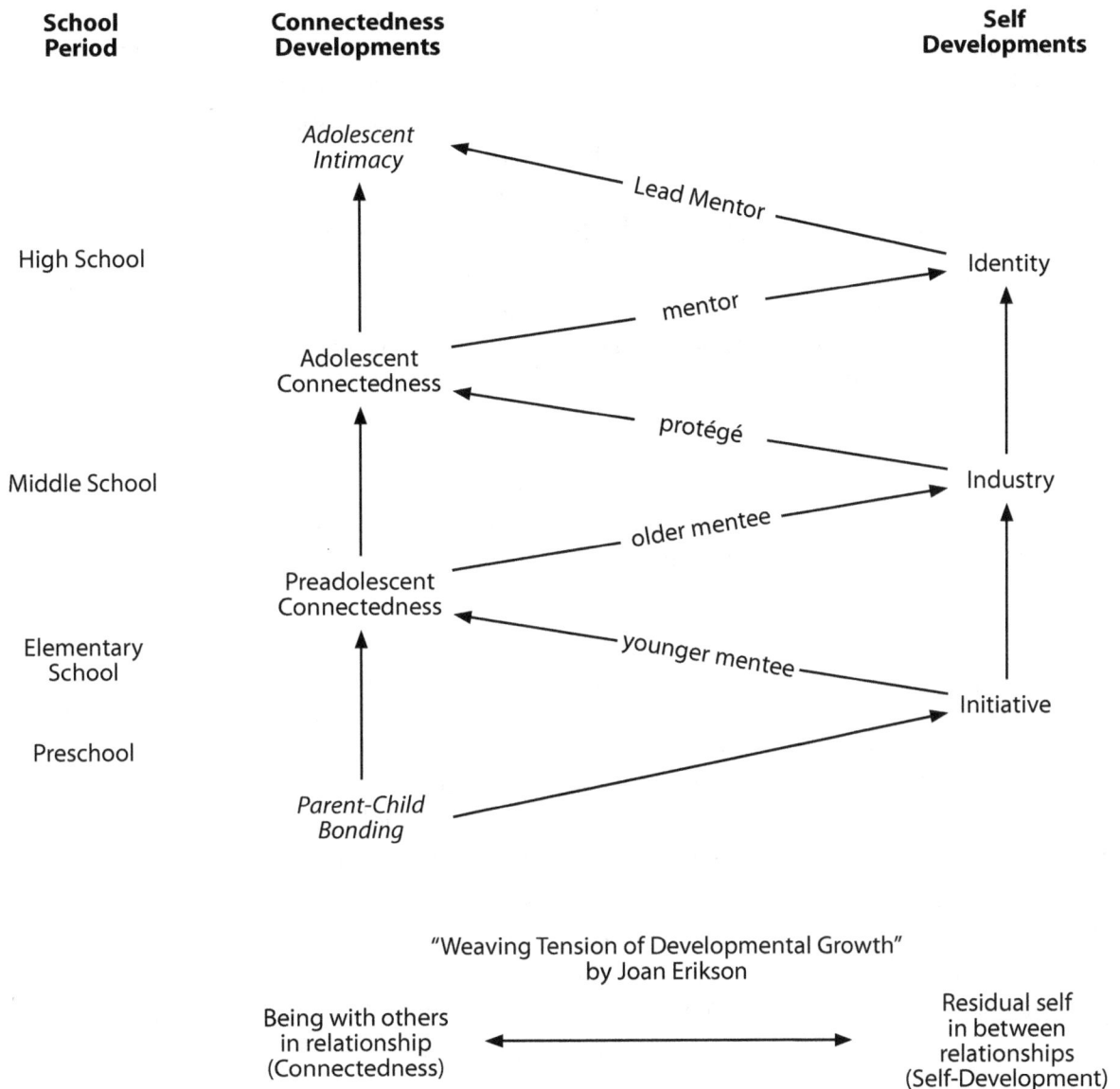

School Period	Connectedness Developments	Self Developments

Adolescent Intimacy

Lead Mentor

High School — Identity

mentor

Adolescent Connectedness

protégé

Middle School — Industry

older mentee

Preadolescent Connectedness

Elementary School

younger mentee

Initiative

Preschool

Parent-Child Bonding

"Weaving Tension of Developmental Growth"
by Joan Erikson

Being with others in relationship (Connectedness) ⟷ Residual self in between relationships (Self-Development)

self-in-the-future. Consideration of the mentor's needs must remain firmly atop the priority list of CAMP coordinators because both mentors and mentees should benefit significantly from CAMP.

Only upon the foundation of two persons' solid identities can intimacy find firm foundation. Only then are both persons "ready for intimacy, that is, the capacity to commit him/herself to concrete affiliations and partnerships and to develop ethical strength to abide by such commitments, even though they may call for significant sacrifices and compromises." (Erikson, 1950, p. 263). The collective culture of positive peer relationships that gets formed in CAMP, as well as the emphasis of mentors' attendance (fidelity) to the program also helps them practice elements of intimacy. But mentors need to understand that their relationship—attempts at intimacy—may be frustrating at times because their mentees do not bring a firm sense of self (achieved identity) into the mentoring relationship. So it will feel one-sided at times.

Finally, well beyond CAMP participation for mentors, but perhaps more reflective of the developmental task of CAMP Coordinators, industry, identity and intimacy come together to form a socially interested metaidentity and a collective intimacy called generativity. "Generativity is primarily the concern with establishing and guiding the next generation … From the crisis of generativity emerges the strength of care" (Erikson, 1995, p. 607). Inchoate expressions of generativity—seeds of care, if you will—are planted in both the mentor and the mentee through effective mentoring relationship. Neither is fully generative at this age, but both may be oriented in that direction as a result of strong, supportive, caring relationships cultivated in the program. Rather, it is the Program Coordinator who best embodies the developmental challenge of generativity in her work.

Stages of connectedness for all people in the program

What we wish to add to this set of key developmental tasks is the need to establish, experience, and successfully manage both earlier and later forms of adolescent connectedness in order to help provide both mentees and mentors a bridge from each of these developmental tasks to the next. It is this principle that informs why CAMP emphasizes connectedness (i.e., the mentoring relationship) over self-development of the individual (e.g., specific skills). At least for some youth, the school provides ample rewards for individual success, for the mastery of individual talents, and for self-examination (or, at least glorification). But far less attention has been paid to the developmental glue called connectedness. It is this connectedness that helps one successfully move from one stage to the next and ultimately experience the strength of care. Therefore it warrants some explication and perhaps illustration of its differing role for mentees and mentors, as is illustrated in the figure below.

Preadolescent connectedness is different from adolescent connectedness largely as a function of the self-developments that inform each. Preadolescent connectedness, for example, does not include as many contexts or differentiated relationships as adolescent connectedness. Preadolescent connectedness to family, school, peers and friends serves as a foundation for the kinds of attitudes, social skills, and self-perceptions that are developed among older mentees (and protégés). But peers are not distinguished from culturally different peers, as they are in adolescent connectedness. Similarly, friends in preadolescence are later differentiated into romantic friends and nonromantic friends.

For older mentees and protégés establishing, experiencing and affirming important connections through the program helps them master social skills, develop a positive attitude towards school, and build self-esteem. For high school students, CAMP affords opportunities to view themselves in novel ways in their search for a cohesive identity. Therefore, the role that CAMP plays in youth development is different for older mentees, protégés, mentors and lead mentors.

Mentees. The fourth-grade mentee may use developmental mentoring to first establish preadolescent connectedness within the ecology of the school, and then to develop social skills, academic achievement/attitudes, and self-esteem (industry). The two steps (as described in Kohut, 1977) of receiving empathy, praise, and attention, and then the development of skills by modeling and internalizing those of an idealized other, provide the two main ingredients of a developmental mentoring relationship for mentees that help promote their connectedness to classmates, teachers and school. These are illustrated in the model below, showing what Kohut called the poles in the tripolar self. Pole one is the creation of ambition through the provision of empathy, praise, and attention. Parents do this, but other people, including mentors, continue to serve a similar role throughout an individual's life. The second pole represents the process by which we come to idealize and prize those who have provided us empathy, praise, and attention within a context of clear, consistent structure. This leads to identification with that person and the adoption of their beliefs, goals, and values. As a result, these relationships shape the trajectories of one's development by influencing the content one's character. The third step or pole is the product of the first two poles: ambition + idealization = opportunities for connectedness, or the experience of twinship, chumship, and affiliation. Out of these relationships of affiliation, such as with peers and friends, one develops skills and talents that

Figure 3. The Relationship Between Connectedness, Self-Development, and in CAMP Roles

Ambition develops through early experiences of feeling valued, active, and loved + **Goals**, ideals, and valuation follow from identifying with those seen as strong, consistent, calm, and good = **Skills and talents** derive from the **ambition** to achieve **goals**

are consistent with their shared values, the role of which is to secure subsequent empathy, praise, and attention from them in predictable ways.

Older mentees (those entering middle school) may utilize the program to capitalize on the strengths (e.g., social skills, school attitudes, self-esteem) they've achieved and move toward establishing a more ecologically broad form of adolescent connectedness; these older mentees often need a formal structure, ideally a prosocial community in which to use or exercise these strengths. Children in middle school who have grown beyond their role as mentee and who are in need of a broader, prosocial, inclusive social network in which to exercise their new self-developments can become protégés.

Protégé. Being a protégé allows the preadolescent to draw on previously developed social skills, school attitudes/achievement, and their budding self-esteem to build a broader form of adolescent connectedness through their cooperative work as an aid to another mentor and mentee. The protégé then affirms this larger sense of adolescent connectedness in a way that propels her identity development processes. This occurs when the protégé uses her new skills to manage and contribute to those new relationships. The protégé's adolescent connectedness (within a larger ecology) is increased when the protégé makes efforts to take others' points of view on their contributions as well as to take an abstracted perspective on the relationship.

Mentor. For teenagers, being a mentor allows them to draw on experiences of prosocial connectedness and to more fully develop their identity through volunteering and by regularly exercising their ability to take another's (third person) perspective on their own actions or on situations. The practice of this somewhat more selfless focus on caring for others (the mentee primarily) likely fosters the ability to achieve deeper levels of intimacy with others. This is why the friendships in preadolescence start to differentiate regular friends and peers from "best friends" and romantic friends. Similarly, a clearer sense of one's ethnic identity and social groups leads to a differentiation of peers and culturally different peers. This widening of the social ecology—which mentors can appreciate but their mentees cannot—is what is afforded to high school aged youth via their expanded social cognitive abilities. New skills in social cognition contribute to the adolescent's widening social ecology of adolescent connectedness. We say more about this in the next section.

Typically, the psychosocial tasks that Erikson describes reflect social opportunities available to youth at different points in their lives. These opportunities greatly depend on a child's place in society, such as her socioeconomic status and cultural group membership. But rather than emphasize the crises to be overcome, we prefer to share some of the Eriksons' writing about development through strengths. For example, "The strength acquired at any stage is tested by the necessity to transcend it in such a way that the individual can take chances in the next stage with what was most vulnerably precious in the previous one" (Erikson, 1950, p. 263).

Joan Erikson, however, has been just as cogent a writer about developmental stages as strengths, and she suggests it is these strengths which propel us into community with others. According to Joan Erikson all strengths from previous stages must be incorporated successfully into the next stage so that the adolescent "may emerge as a unique individual with a sense of pride and trust in unique capacities and a sense of active competence with which a personal environment can be shaped or reshaped" (Erikson, 1988, p. 96).

In Figure 4, we illustrate one way of thinking about connectedness in terms of Eriksonian stages. The figure combines Kegan's (1982) developmental helix and Joan Erikson's concept of a woven tension of developmental strengths. In Erik Erikson's work, there is perhaps an undue emphasis on self-developments, and too little attention to the development of connectedness—of intimacy, connection, cooperation and dependency—particularly among children and adolescents.

But attachment theory makes it an incontestable fact that we depend on our connectedness at one stage—that strength of relationships to direct and define oneself—to propel us toward the next set of self-development strengths. Without new forms of connectedness resulting from our progression through each set of strengths (stages), the self that develops would be without any purpose beyond itself. It would be hollow, likely shallow, and perhaps directionless. Indeed, Kohut (1977) suggests that without empathy, praise, and attention (which must occur with a relationship with important others) individuals would lack motivation, the capacity and desire to achieve each new developmental strength.

Kohut's Developmental Model

For the program to have an effect on mentors' and mentees' connectedness to school, peers, their futures and themselves, some degree of empathy must be cultivated between mentor and mentee that leads the mentee to want to internalize the mentor's values, behaviors, and interests (Kohut, 1977). Kohut suggests that it is empathy, praise and attention that leads individuals (particularly youth) to identify with and model the behaviors of others whom they hold in high esteem. This approach is illustrated in the graphic presented earlier. Given that it is his formulation that serves as the basis of the CAMP training's emphasis on these three keys to promoting self-development, it is further fleshed out below.

Part I—Empathy, praise, and attention. The fundamental building block for self-developments and connectedness more generally is the provision of empathy, praise, and attention. These critical elements form the foundation of the main self-developments—self-esteem, identity, and a future orientation. Kohut, a psychoanalyst and the founder of self psychology, explains that the first and most primary need in life is for empathy, praise, and attention (EPA). Each interpersonal interaction that provides EPA fosters healthy connectedness. So, mentors must work hard to be sure their mentees experience genuine empathy, praise, and attention (EPA) from themselves and others in the program.

Part II—Clear, consistent structure. Second, the youth must experience three additional elements that build on empathy, praise and attention: Clear, consistent structure. To this end, CAMP will only work if empathic, attentive, and praising mentors work within a structure that affords the following:

1. Clearly defined examples of desirable behaviors, and ideally these should be consistently modeled by adults whom the adolescent sees as competent and emotionally supportive

2. Both opportunities and coaching necessary to develop skills just beyond his or her level of knowledge and competence

3. The belief or perception that these behaviors will result in better relationships and more fun at school and at home

Based on this theory, we train mentors to provide ample empathy praise and attention, and we work hard to structure a program that provides clear, consistent, and developmentally supportive structure.

Although it is a fundamental and basic phenomenon, it is important to realize that the ability to be empathic toward another individual does not always come naturally. Children without a stable and supportive caregiver, and especially those who have been abused, may not fully develop their capacity to feel empathy for others. Therefore, it is likely that youth referred to mentoring programs because

Figure 4. Developmental Tasks for Youth

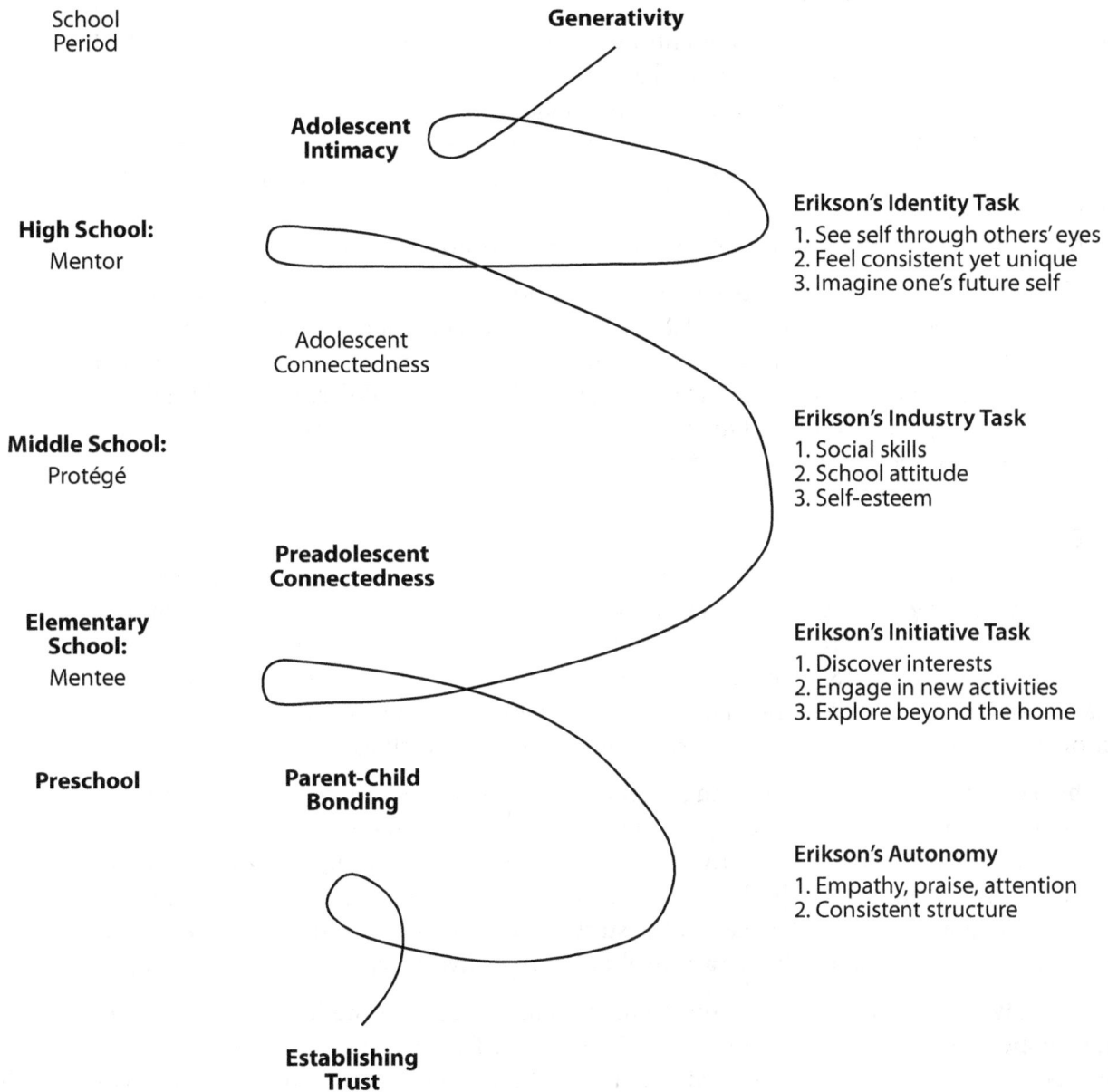

School
Period

Generativity

**Adolescent
Intimacy**

Erikson's Identity Task
1. See self through others' eyes
2. Feel consistent yet unique
3. Imagine one's future self

High School:
Mentor

Adolescent
Connectedness

Middle School:
Protégé

Erikson's Industry Task
1. Social skills
2. School attitude
3. Self-esteem

**Preadolescent
Connectedness**

**Elementary
School:**
Mentee

Erikson's Initiative Task
1. Discover interests
2. Engage in new activities
3. Explore beyond the home

Preschool

**Parent-Child
Bonding**

Erikson's Autonomy
1. Empathy, praise, attention
2. Consistent structure

**Establishing
Trust**

"Weaving Tension of Developmental Growth"
by Joan Erikson

Being with others
in relationship
(Connectedness)
⟷
Residual self
in between
relationships
(Self-Development)

of their difficult home environments or their aggressive behavior with peers may have a harder time learning to be empathic.

Fortunately, there is considerable evidence that empathy is a skill that can be developed and learned if properly instructed. That said, it is also quite likely that the best way to learn empathy is to experience it first-hand, to have it modeled by those whom we hold in high regard, and to both experience and observe it in relationship. That is why we must train mentors to be empathic, not just train them to teach empathy skills to their mentees.

Participation in the program helps students develop a sense of connectedness that should, in turn, help them to reach the next developmental stage. Awareness of the stage that the student—mentor or mentee—currently inhabits is important for understanding what can or cannot be expected of each within the context of the program. Mentors especially will benefit from understanding how their mentees view the world and what they expect of relationships. The *CAMP Mentor Handbook* and *Training Guide* introduce a number of activities designed to help mentors grasp these concepts, which should aid mentors in building strong, empathic relationships with their mentees.

We feel empathy is the key to effective mentoring (Rhodes, 2002). Empathy consists of understanding another's feelings while maintaining a clear boundary between self and others which permits an individual to experience another's affect while maintaining the meaning of that person's experience. The structure of the format used in CAMP actually follows from a developmental theory of perspective-taking that also is used to train mentors and youth to be more interpersonally effective. This theory is described in the next section.

Perspective-taking

What we try to convey next in this chapter is how cognitive-developmental theory is used to structure the mentoring interactions, and how it provides a "developmental" approach through a series of interpersonal interactions that mimic the development of social skills across the lifespan. Understanding the role of Selman's (1980) developmental theory of perspective-taking level in what we call "walking up the developmental ladder" will help Program Coordinators and their Lead Mentors know how to structure each part of the mentoring meetings.

This theory of perspective-taking—and specifically how its stages prescribe the order and nature of the activities planned for each meeting—is described first in the section below. However, the theory also supports the use of reflection activities that we think serve to strengthen the relationship (and the program) and help ensure that both participants leave the relationship better than when they entered it. These reflection activities take place at the start and end of each meeting, and they are described in the second half of this chapter. These are all about perspective sharing in the relationship.

CAMP Sandwich. One metaphor for the mentor-mentee meeting time sequence that we explain using perspective-taking theory is of a CAMP sandwich. The two slices of bread are reflection activities. The first reflection is designed to help each share their separate point of view with the other. Here they learn what has gone on in each other's life in the prior week—the ups and downs. At the end of the hour they reflect on their shared perspective, their time together.

3-2-1 Activity and Reflections. The first activity is called the 3-2-1 activity, and the second activity is called the Activity Reflection. What is learned from both is kept on record in service of a fun, rewarding activity done quarterly called the Newly Matched game. In between these two slices of reflection is a sequence of interactions that is based on the developmental theory described below.

Robert Selman (1980) presents a model of perspective taking which reveals that between the early years of elementary school to the end of high school, there is a developmental progression in the complexity with which individuals are able to take the perspective of others. This progression means mentees and mentors are likely to view the world very differently. This fact has considerable implications for training mentors to understand that they will see the world, themselves, and their mentees differently than their mentees see the world, themselves, and their mentors.

Selman and Schultz (1990) have emphasized the important interrelationship between cognitive perspective-taking ability and interpersonal behaviors or skills. In other words, how the complexity of the mentor and mentee's thinking will shape the manner of their interactions and thereby influence the course of their relationship. The elementary-aged child, for example, tends to act impulsively because he or she has only a limited awareness that his or her wants differ from others. She cannot as easily consider two, opposing points of view simultaneously, especially in moments of decision-making and action. Understanding the source of the mentee's impulsivity can help the mentor better avoid stereotyping the mentee (e.g., according to race or class) and can lessen the inevitable frustration that results in such moments by helping the mentor depersonalize the mentee's impulsive acts. During the elementary years, children become able to articulate their own points of view, and by the end of elementary school most youth are able to hold in their mind another's point of view—that is, another's wants, needs, and feelings.

For many youth in elementary school it is hard to give equal merit to others' points of view and therefore they are not compelled to cooperate or concede their immediate wants and needs. The challenge for youth in middle school is to effectively act in ways that demonstrate the ability to negotiate between their own and others' wants and needs. This movement from unilateral assertiveness to a cooperativeness through the coordination of two people's separate needs ushers in the developmental importance of a "best friend" or "chum" as described by Sullivan (1953) and summarized in Table 1.

The developmental inclination to develop a chumship is a good example of the importance of preadolescent connectedness that is primarily dyadic in nature, nonromantic, and which allows opportunities to establish trust in relationships outside the home. Typically the chumship is the first relationship youth have in which they are willing to fully disclose their inner life and trust that their confidants, or chums, will honor their secrets and not betray them. Out of this chumship can develop an appreciation for "the relationship" as well as a sense of caring for and trust in one's peers. For some youth, their mentors may provide their first opportunity to form such a chumship. If the mentor is consistent, safe, empathic and interested, the youth may confide in the mentor (achieve a degree of trust) in ways that allow them to practice those skills for later use with friends and eventually romantic partners.

Table 1. A Look at Developmental Differences and a Way to Understand Them

Children (4–8-year-olds) need to have an adult audience to attend to their play and notice achievements. One of the most important roles played by others is to provide empathy, praise, and attention to establish a strong sense of self.

Juveniles (9–10-year-olds) need help to manage competition, cooperation, and compromise. Many mentees will not have totally refined these skills yet and need help. They will be identifying their unique skills and abilities, and need to be encouraged to try new things, and they appreciate praise for their successes.

Preadolescents (11–13-year-olds) seek out a nonsexual (typically same-sex) confidant, a chum or intimate and are looking to spend time with those with whom they share interests and beliefs. They will start forming in-out groups, and may need help entering groups (avoiding being left out) or venturing outside of their close dyadic friendship. So structuring group interactions, as done in CAMP, is very helpful.

Adolescents (14–17-year-olds) want to discover who they are uniquely and may want to find a sexually intimate (ultimately, a collaborative and loving) relationship. Their self-assessments may be critical and feel embarrassing. Socially teens are starting to see how their interests, beliefs, and activity choices result in group memberships. This "group" mentality can be utilized or harnessed in the CAMP by creating a cohesive program culture. Teens left alone may organize themselves in superficial groupings and model deviant behavior to impress one another. Trying to help teens think about their beliefs and be able to share and discuss them is one unique opportunity that CAMP presents teens through the use of the curriculum and encouragements to have mentors model their thinking and self-understanding to mentees.

By the high school years, youth tend to become better at seeing their needs and wants from a third-person point of view. This allows them to recognize others' needs and wants, and their willingness to care for others propels them to engage in behaviors (interpersonal negotiation strategies) that help others in their pursuits, even if it means deferring their own individual needs (Selman & Schultz, 1990). This has very positive effects on their ongoing relationships.

This series of cognitive-developments—from egocentrism, through first-, second-, and third-person perspective taking—informs the kinds of behaviors that youth engage in with their mentees as well as with their peers, parents, and teachers. This developmental sequence of levels of perspective coordination and the interpersonal behavior each level supports is illustrated in Table 2. The table also illustrates two different interpersonal orientations—self-transforming and other-transforming. Some children transform their own needs in moments of conflict or interpersonal resistance, while some try to persuade others to accommodate their needs. Whether a child acts more self-transforming or other-transforming in interactions also will shape the nature of their interactions.

Table 2. Social Perspective Taking and Interpersonal Negotiation Strategies (INS)

Perspective-taking: INS	Examples of INS for the two interpersonal orientations	
	Self-transforming	Other-transforming
3rd-person: Collaborative (Emerges in ages 13–15)	Collaboration; acting out of shared needs & concern for "us." Here actions are considered for their effects on the relationship. The "we" perspective is given primacy over individual perspectives.	
2nd-person: Reciprocal (Dominant in ages 9–12)	Ask why, barter, go second	Argue, persuade, go first
1st-person: Unilateral (Dominant in ages 5–9)	Obey, give in, acquiesce	Dictate, bully, order, tell
Egocentric: Impulsive	Whine, flee, hide	Fight, grab, hit

The fact that mentors and mentees bring different levels of perspective-taking skills to the relationship influences the depth and nature of conversations children and adolescents can engage in with each other. When brought to bear on cross-age peer mentoring, it becomes clear that the child mentee and adolescent mentor see and act in the world in different ways, each of which can affect the development of a mutually satisfying interpersonal relationship.

In the CAMP training materials, the skills and experiences that are provided are intended to help the mentors think about the developmental needs of the mentees in order to tailor their interactions accordingly. Within each summer the developmental curriculum focuses on one of three connectedness themes that guide the teaching of mentees in all three grades in the program (4, 5, and 6), but each of the three grades of mentees may have slightly different developmental needs. The rising fifth-graders are just coming to understand ways in which people are governed by personalities that define them as different and unique; so working with the fifth-grader can be directed toward self connectedness. In grade 6, children are becoming more interested in social interactions and in their ability to effectively navigate them. So grade 6 classes can focus on social interactions and skills.

Protégés also bring different cognitive-developmental agendas and abilities to their work. By grade 7, children are beginning to think abstractly, and with this cognitive development they become able to understand social systems. For example, abstract thinking leads to the ability to see systems of influence, such as those processes that comprise the memberships to ethnic, class, and other social groups. They also start to see how individuals influence systems and vice-versa. By helping the seventh-graders think about the interactions and systems that make up society, connectedness to society can be most successfully incorporated. That is, most fifth-graders are not ready for this type of discussion, but many grade 7 and 8 students crave it. The curriculum we have developed allows for one shared summer theme that can be taught across these three developmental periods, and efforts by the Program Coordinator and the mentors need to tailor the use of those materials to suit the needs of the mentees.

This theoretical model is used to guide the connectedness to reading curriculum in the spring, so it is important that Program Coordinators and Lead Mentors effectively teach this model to mentors through training so that they can use it effectively at that time. For this reason, this model also is the focus of the third main mentor training. We use this mentor training to help the mentors both understand some of the developmental differences between them and their mentees as well as to help the mentors develop a different language (the "Language of the Animals on the Yumewii Mountain") for discussing interpersonal behaviors and problem solving with their mentees, as is done in the connectedness to reading curriculum activity.

Developmental activity sequence: Walking matches up the developmental ladder

Probably one of the most unique elements of the program is the use of Selman's developmental theory of perspective-taking skills and corresponding interpersonal negotiation strategies to structure the mentoring activities described in Chapter 6. This theory of social perspective coordination is used in several ways. It provides content and the main model used for the springtime connectedness to reading curriculum. It also is used to provide a structure for the two hour meetings after school.

Walking up the developmental ladder. When structuring the hour and a half the mentors and mentees spend together one-on-one (either after school, on SuperSaturdays, or during blocks of time during the summer program), we use a plan of events that "walks the mentor and mentee up the developmental ladder." By walking up the developmental ladder, we mean that we escort the match through the four stages of social perspective coordination—from physicalistic (egocentric, level 0) interactions, to unilateral (self-sharing, level 1) interchanges between the two about what's happened in their lives since last meeting, to cooperative (self-reflective and perspective coordinating, level 2) activities that link multiple points of view, to a culminating activity designed to help them focus on their relationship, their shared perspective (level 3).

This means the match (0) engages in a physical icebreaker, (1) each shares something about themselves, (2) they use information about one another or the instructions provided for a task to cooperate in a learning activity, and finally (3) there is an effort to strengthen their relationship so they see beyond themselves as individuals and come to better appreciate themselves as members of a relationship that endures over time and that has a life of its own.

This last concept, however, can only be understood well by the mentor. It is too developmentally complex for the mentee to really understand the "life of their relationship," so instead it is the mentor's responsibility to help the mentee experience interpersonally what the mentee cannot comprehend cognitively. By doing this, the mentor coaches the mentee into what Vygotsky (1978) calls a zone of proximal development. The mentor helps the mentee participate in ways of being that she cannot yet experience on her own without help, but which she will later be able to do independently as a teen will be able to do, having experienced it first in this close relationship, chumship, or friendship (Sullivan, 1953).

What we are attempting to do during the mentoring meetings is walk the matches through these developmental levels, from the bottom level up, in an attempt to push their capacity for social perspective coordination during the connectedness curriculum activities. This is very similar to what Allen Ivey describes counselors doing in his *Developmental Therapy* (1986), but using a different developmental theorist's model. Where he uses Piaget's stages, we rely on Selman's perspective-taking levels because perspective-taking is such an essential skill for effective interpersonal relations, and it is, as we suggested in Chapter 2, what propels growth in adolescent connectedness.

The TEAM Framework

Initially, we referred to CAMP as a "developmental mentoring" program because of the emphasis placed on developmental theory and principles to guide program outcomes and processes as described above. However, as described later in this chapter, we learned that "developmental" mentoring has its own connotation in the mentoring field as a result of the pioneering work of Morrow and Styles (1995). But our program also uses skill-development curricular activities in ways that make it resemble an instrumental approach that focuses on skill and character development, as defined by Hamilton and Hamilton (2005). While CAMP is inherently more developmental than instrumental, at least in that it starts with a heavy relationship focus, we hope to make clear that these two approaches are two sides of the same collaborative, youth-centered approach. Therefore, to associate CAMP only with the "developmental" approach vis-à-vis Morrow and Styles' characterization may be both limiting and misleading.

Understanding the programmatic emphasis on relational, playful and collaborative interactions as characterized in the Theoretically Evolving Activities in Mentoring (TEAM) Framework described in this chapter should help facilitate mentor training, curriculum development, and those on-the-fly decisions that have to get made in response to the question, "What do I do now?"

Even though most of the interactions that take place in the program are somewhat scripted by the curriculum or structured by the developmental "up the ladder" sequence of activities (as described in Chapter 7), the moment-to-moment interactions are guided by the mentor and mentee themselves. Both will likely have some confusion about what a mentor is, what a mentee is, and how they should interact. We believe that training mentors in appropriate roles can be done through a discussion of the two main types of mentoring approaches in the field—the instrumental and developmental relationship styles—as well as through analysis of the focus, purpose and authorship of mentoring activities. The main point of these discussions is to illustrate that even when an activity seems very straight forward, mentors will need to make decisions about whether they are going to be serious or playful, relational or goal-directed, and collaborative or unilateral. Understanding the consequences of these decisions will help make the mentors better decision makers in the group, in the moment.

Understandings of the relationship

As discussed earlier, a mentor sees the mentoring relationship in a different way than the mentee does, partly due to their differing development stages and perspective taking abilities, and partly due to the circumstances surrounding the formation of the relationship. We often see mentors who want to offer guidance, and lead the mentee toward adulthood. Yet the mentee may want something quite different: a companion to play with and confide in. These differing expectations are not universally held, but are quite common. Research has shown that many mentors who feel that the mentoring relationship is not helping the mentee reach some specific goals are less likely to continue to invest in the relationship, and may skip meetings or drop out of the program. On the other hand, mentees who feel the relationship is primarily focused on academics, behavior issues, or some other conventional adult goals are less likely to offer the trust that is necessary for the relationship to develop. Only within the bond of friendship can the mentee develop a sense of connectedness and practice taking the perspective of others. There is often a tension between the desires of the participants, but successful mentoring relationships manage to strike a balance: a genuine friendship within which the mentee can acquire interpersonal, academic, and other skills.

As will be seen in the following discussion, there are several ways to help mentors work toward this balance. The simplest is to make sure that the mentors understand that developing a trusting relationship with an older peer is in fact a very significant step toward adulthood for many youth. What may seem like an aimless relationship to the mentor can actually be a crucial developmental step for a young person who may not have many close, trusting relationships.

Helping mentors to see that a fun, playful activity can actually constitute emotional work which helps build self-esteem, trust, and a sense of personal identity in the mentee is often enough to bridge the gap between a mentor who wants to make a difference and a mentee who wants to have fun. As Harry Stack Sullivan posited, the best-friend relationship that youth start to develop in elementary school prefigures later romantic relationships, and is crucial to developing a positive sense of self-worth (Sullivan, 1953). If mentors can develop a relationship with their mentee that is somewhere between a best friend (or "chum" as Sullivan refers to it) and a role model, they have a chance to make a real difference.

Naturally, the mentors need to bring this understanding of the relationship into practice. By being careful to observe the state of the relationship, the mood and inclinations of the youth, and the nature of the curriculum activities, mentors can make good decisions about how to implement the activities in the context of a developing relationship. In order to do this, we encourage mentors to think about the implementation of activities (even games or conversations) using three criteria: focus, purpose, and authorship (see Karcher & Nakkula, 2010 for a more detailed description). The first thing to keep in mind is that different relationships will develop with a different focus, which is most pronounced in the early stages of the relationship.

Focus: relational or goal-oriented

The focus of a mentoring interaction is determined by whether it is essentially relational or goal-directed. For instance, if a mentor spends most of a session working through the steps of a curriculum activity with his mentee, we would consider this a goal-directed interaction. A relational interaction, on the other hand, might be a long conversation about the mentee's friends at school, or her relationship with her parents. We call relationships that tend to develop best within the context of goal-directed activities instrumental relationships, while those that flourish without many artificial goals are referred to as developmental. Both are described in depth below, but before getting into the intricacies of these relationship styles, we want to emphasize that both are healthy and normal in a mentoring program. The key is recognizing what the mentee's needs are, and implementing the CAMP curriculum with the appropriate focus for each individual relationship.

The instrumental approach

One pair of pioneers in the field of youth mentoring is Steven and Mary Agnes Hamilton at Cornell University. Their work studying apprenticeships (Hamilton & Hamilton, 1992), primarily among high school aged adolescents, gave us the term "instrumental," which has become synonymous with healthy goal-focused mentoring relationships (in contrast to the "prescriptive" style described by Morrow & Styles, 1995, below). The instrumental approach is important because of its focus on observable goals which may help teen mentors feel more efficacious (see Karcher, Herrera, & Hansen, 2010).

The Hamiltons found those who saw their primary purpose as developing a relationship with their mentees were least likely to meet regularly, whereas "the mentors who seemed best able to overcome the frustrations of their task were those who combined the aims of developing competence and developing character" (Hamilton & Hamilton, 1992, p. 548). For this reason, the Hamiltons suggest that mentoring for high school-aged youth is more appealing to youth and more effective when "it occurs in the context of joint goal-directed (instrumental) activity" and when "the relationship develops around shared goals and actions more than purely social interaction." (Hamilton & Hamilton, 2005, p. 352–353).

Yet another, equally viable, and in some ways more traditional Big Brothers and Big Sisters–style of mentoring does exactly that. It starts off with a heavy reliance on social interaction, interpersonal discussion, and the activities of listening to and learning about each other.

Developmental relationships

"These relationships were given the label 'developmental' because the adult partner in the match focused on providing youth with a comfort zone in which to address a broad range of developmental tasks—such as building emotional well-being, developing social skills, or gaining straightforward exposure to a range of recreational and cultural activities. Developmental volunteers responded flexibly to their youth, adjusting to any preconceived notions as to the reality, circumstances and needs of their younger partner. Furthermore, these volunteers intentionally incorporated youth into decision-making about the relationship, allowing them to help choose activities and have a voice in determining whether and when the adult would provide advice and guidance." (Morrow & Styles, 1995, p. 19)

Morrow and Styles (1995) characterized mentoring relationships as of two types: developmental relationships and prescriptive relationships. Developmental relationships are characterized by flexibility on behalf of the mentors in that the focus is on development rather than goal attainment. From the onset of the relationship emphasis is placed on establishing a strong connection with the mentee. This sense of connectedness is the primary objective of the mentoring, despite the long-term goals of greater self-esteem, academic achievement, and vocational success. Although mentors in these relationships want their mentees to improve in school, the mentors invest most of their time and effort in developing a reliable, trusting relationship. The mentors are open to expand the scope of their effort only after the relationship is solidified (Morrow, & Styles, 1995). Connection to the mentor is considered the means by which all other connections are encouraged: connectedness to self, others, academics, and their future. Developmental relationships tend to elicit commitment to the relationship from both the mentor and the mentee and can usher change through the sharing of identifications, values, and interests.

Prescriptive relationships

Prescriptive matches are like instrumental matches gone awry. Prescriptive relationships are different in that the mentor tends to dictate the directions of the relationship toward the fulfillment of some prescribed goals, such as improving academic achievement, increases in knowledge, or behavioral changes that are dictated by a program, agency or funder. Such mentors establish the goals, set the pace of the relationship, and focus on specific activities that are deemed critical to achieving specific goals. In response to pressures to shape the mentee in some prescribed way, these mentors tend to resist modifying their expectations, because they are derived from top-down program prescriptions; this can result in frustration, alienation, and disconnection (Morrow, & Styles, 1995). Conversely, mentors who proceed with a more developmental approach are most likely to achieve their primary goal of developing a mutually transformative, development-promoting relationship.

What is important to note, however, is that the developmental and instrumental styles are essentially similar, and differ largely in the types of interaction focus they begin with. The developmental style starts off heavily interpersonal and social, but later shifts attention to addressing problems and concerns that youth brings up. Conversely, the instrumental style starts off well structured around a goal or activity (like our connectedness curriculum activities), without which the pair might feel uncomfortable or awkward. This is more common for boys than girls, it seems. But even these highly goal-oriented matches shift over time, allowing a naturally deepening relationship based on trust, reciprocity and shared interest to develop. Both styles, it should be noted, are characterized by a youth-centeredness and the mentor's active efforts to collaborate and partner with the mentee in the coconstruction of their relationship.

Implications for CAMP

Awareness of these two approaches is helpful for understanding and promoting specific communication patterns among mentors and mentees. Some mentees will be more willing to talk about interpersonal issues right from the beginning. They may confide in their mentors about problems with their parents, siblings, or friends, and thus start to develop an emotional bond with their mentors early on. For these mentees, a developmental approach is best.

 What this means in the context of the program is that intensive curriculum activities are deemphasized, especially if they are seen as getting in the way of the development of the relationship. The activities are still present, of course. But these pairs may move through the activities quickly, or may not complete all of them, as their relationships develop more easily and fully through open-ended conversation or playful interactions. As these relationships become more established, they may find that the curriculum offers techniques for dealing with interpersonal problems. At this point, the emotional bond developed earlier provides a platform for using the tools offered by the curriculum to work on specific interpersonal or emotional problems. In other words, the relationship becomes more goal-oriented.

On the other hand, some mentees will not be emotionally available to the mentor early on in the program. For these youth, it is best to use a more instrumental approach, as the concrete goals of the curriculum activities provide a structure within which to develop trust. As these pairs work through the intellectual and physical challenges of the activities, their emotional bond should grow stronger. The focus at this point is not on developing the relationship directly, but on reaching the goals set out by the activities. When the youth starts to reach a level of trust, the mentor can begin to take a more relational approach. Because they have put in the time and energy, and worked as a team to solve challenges set forth by the program, they can then begin to address problems set forth by the mentee's life. This process may take a long time if the mentee has not experienced many close, trusting relationships before. The mentor should continue to work through activities with her mentee, and look for the signs that the mentee is ready for a more open relationship, and thus a more relational approach.

In both of these scenarios, the mentor needs to take cues from the mentee. If the mentor insists on moving through the curriculum in a rigid way when the mentee wants to spend time developing a relationship, a mentee who had been somewhat emotionally available may begin to shut down and become distant, sensing that the mentor is not interested in a caring relationship. On the other hand, a mentor who moves too quickly into a relational approach may be seen as prying—or even "creepy"—by the mentee who needs some time to develop trust. The mentee may begin to act out or become uncooperative because he sees the mentor as untrustworthy. This is why a prescriptive approach is almost always bad for the relationship. Apart from the stated goals of the program or the day's curriculum activity, each relationship has its own needs, and its own pace. The relationship is like a dance, with the mentor leading, but also paying attention to the mentee's movements so that they don't stray beyond the mentee's relational abilities or comfort zone.

Perception of the activities may be as important as the actual nature of the activities themselves. Let's go back to the idea that mentors often want to engage in instrumental activities (to feel that they are "making a difference") even when what a mentee needs most is a developmental approach. An implication for programmatic training is that when instrumentality is present but downplayed (or clearly embedded in the relationship) it may be most effective. Helping mentors understand that relationship-building is a valid goal can help them see relational interactions as instrumental, and conversely introducing goal-oriented activities in a playful way can help mentees feel more comfortable and engaged.

There is growing evidence that this balanced focus on both instrumental and developmental interactions is essential (e.g., Langhout, Rhodes, & Osborne, 2004; Larose, Cyrenne, Garceau, Brodeur, & Tarabulsy, 2010; Nakkula & Harris, 2010). Morrow and Styles have referred to this as a "hybrid approach." Sometimes this occurs naturally, and sometimes it can be facilitated through programmatic efforts.

To understand this better, the Theoretically Evolving Activities in Mentoring (TEAM) framework was developed to encourage programs to help mentors think about the three characteristics that differentiate these two effective styles, the instrumental and developmental:

1. Focus—how directive they are being (developmental is less, instrumental is more directive)
2. Purpose—adult, conventional, future-oriented goals or playful, fun, youth-oriented goals
3. Authorship—who selects the activity and conversation topics and how?

Purpose: adult-centered or youth-centered

The purpose of an interaction, as opposed to the focus, refers to how conventional (adult-oriented) it is. Doing homework or talking about behavior problems is considered an adult-oriented interaction, while playing a game or talking about a TV show would be more youth-oriented. Whether an interaction in a match is relational (i.e., focused primarily on the relationship or on the child's inner experience) or goal-oriented (i.e., focused primarily on the achievement of some objective outcome) may be independent of the interaction's purpose. Learning to fly a kite is fun and fulfills the child's purpose needs, but it also is goal-oriented if the focus is on the mentee's need to learn the necessary steps in getting a kite to stay up in the air. Here, the purpose is the child's need for fun and mastery of a skill valued mostly by children (not a conventionally valued goal). Indeed, Karcher, Herrera, and Hansen (2010) report sports, games, and crafts activities appeared most effective in leveraging strong relationships. This provides evidence that structured interactions may reflect a relational focus. Conversely, the same activity may reflect a goal-oriented focus if attainment of an observable outcome trumps a relationship focus.

Karcher, Herrera, and Hansen (2010) report that high levels of academic activities in school-based mentoring—especially early in the match—can be harmful to the mentoring relationship and can inhibit the potential of such efforts. Their studies suggest novice mentors may be more vulnerable than trained mentoring program staff to perceived expectations of other stakeholders in the youth's development (such as teachers), particularly the expectation that they (the mentors) should engage their mentees in academically focused activities. As a result, mentors can shift their focus away from relationship-building and toward an overly structured, goal-oriented, task-focused approach, without considering the needs of the mentee. When this happens, the matches more often fail— both ending prematurely, with attendant frustrations, and in terms of not reaching their potential impact. This problem seems to be even more pronounced when teens mentor children. Teens are cognitively limited in their ability to fully appreciate the power of the relationship itself, and they might feel particularly obligated to fulfill their "mature" or conventional responsibilities—namely to ensure their mentee's academic success. The result can be an overemphasis on goal-oriented interactions in matches, and this seems to happen more with both less experienced, poorly trained, and unsupervised mentors as well as with teen mentors.

Although the purpose of mentoring matches often reflects the conventions of adult society, such conversations can be "relational" if the focus is on internal processes in the child or strengthening the relationship (rather than engaging in it primarily to achieve an objective outcome). Quite often, however, conventional conversations with a conventional (adult-world) purpose are oriented toward affecting the child's future behavior by giving instructions or trying to build specific skills or attitudes, and therefore are more goal-oriented even though they directly inform the child's development of skills and competence. With age, children are increasingly interested in developing skills that reflect the conventions of adult society (and that are not really youthful or playful), and such activities can be experienced positively by the youth. But if the child is not open to such a conventional activity, then the match may be undermined and unable to create a high-quality relationship. Such is the case in the prescriptive mentoring style with its goal orientation but lack of youth-centeredness (or collaboration).

Consider that different mentor-mentee pairs within a given program can appear to take on several purposes, ranging from having fun and being friendly to being serious and studious. Sometimes mentors vary in their purpose because they are flexible and follow their mentee's lead, noticing what the mentee seems to need at different points in the relationship. Sometimes, however, mentors are confused, and their varying purpose reflects a grasping effort to do whatever comes to mind in the moment. These mentors' differing assumptions about the purpose of their work are readily observable by program staff and provide opportunities for staff support and ongoing training. Monitoring the mentor's sense of purpose is essential for program staff, because outcomes of a given mentoring relationship are often mediated by the purpose in mentor-mentee interactions.

If a playful purpose (and one that is collaboratively decided upon or authored) is at the core of mentoring, it is interesting that normative "peer pressure" to have fun and be playful may be the primary catalyst of this program's effectiveness. This certainly is likely the case in the program where most mentor-mentee interactions occur in the presence of peers.

Authorship: unilateral or collaborative

One emerging story line is that it may not be whether or how to structure mentoring, or even who structures the mentor-mentee relationship, but the characteristic manner in which the mentors and their mentees negotiate their interactions—for what reasons, in what way, and toward what or whose ends. While it is important for programs to be "structured" by mentoring staff and professionals, those programs in which mentors come up with their own structure or programs in which the mentees are the determining partner in deciding what occurs in the match, both seem to fall short (Karcher, Herrera, & Hansen, 2010). One of the lessons we have learned is that the way in which match activities, discussions, and interactions are negotiated or authored is fundamental to match success.

Given that collaboration—viewed by Selman and Schultz (1990) as the ability to act in accordance with (or in response to) multiple competing social perspectives—is a more developmentally complex task, mentors of children may have to create collaboration largely by their own efforts. Similarly, mentors of challenging or resistant teenage mentees may require more creativity and flexibility to effectively foster collaboration within their relationships or around specific instrumental tasks. For older adolescent mentors, who are more cognitively advanced, it may be easier to interact collaboratively than it is for their mentees. Therefore, mentors and protégés will need training, coaching, and reminding that their efforts to be collaborative may not always be reciprocated and may even result in the mentee taking advantage of them. This is normal, and needs to be explained to mentors, especially when mentors and their mentees differ in their social class or race, so that this developmental difference is not mistaken for a cultural difference that would be unfavorable to the mentees. In the Instrumental approach, as exemplified by the Hamiltons' work (Hamilton & Hamilton, 1992; 2005), the mentor not only teaches skills but attends to the outer and inner life of the mentee and expresses concern (albeit, secondary to the skills training) such that this becomes the apprenticeship mentor, who guides the mentee in work and life skills.

This approach is consistent with a cognitive-developmental view of such interactions as including multiple social perspectives—requiring a "we" perspective or accommodation of mentee and mentee, which we described above in the discussion of Selman's work (Selman 1980; Selman & Schultz, 1990). By contrast, in the Tutor approach (Table 3, cell 7), one person in the match wants these adult skills and seeks or provides them unilaterally. It is not always that the mentor pushes the skills approach characteristic of the tutor role. Sometimes the mentee only wants skills, not a friendship, and this can be disconcerting to the mentee. In fact, if the mentee wanted these skills but the mentor did not plan on teaching these skills (e.g., did not think that is what a "mentor" was supposed to do), there would be a unilateral effort by the youth to gain adult-world skills from the mentor. The mentee might even resist the mentor being more "Instrumental" by rejecting the mentor's efforts to get to know the youth's inner and home life and by ignoring the mentor's gestures at empathy or playfulness. This may be experienced by the mentor as a rejection by the mentee, when in fact it reflects a conflict in their sense of purpose, and a lack of collaboration to overcome that conflict.

In Table 3, collaboratively negotiated mentoring activities with a shared purpose are located in the center column. In this way, there may really be three types of mentoring interaction purposes. The activity or discussion content can serve two somewhat one-sided purposes, either for achieving goals that are adult-related or reflect the mentor's agenda (left column) or for having fun and doing something intrinsically motivating to the mentee (right column). But sometimes an activity or interaction can meet both the mentor's and the mentee's needs, resulting in a mutual or shared purpose. We feel that any research that examines focus and purpose of the interactions (e.g., using reported activities from an activity log to predict outcomes or relationship quality), but does not consider the degree of collaborative authorship, will always be vulnerable to an alternative explanation.

Table 3. The TEAM View of Mentoring Relationship Interactions: Focus, Purpose, and Authorship

Purpose	Unilateral Authorship: a "me" or mentor focused	Collaborative Authorship (collaboration)	Unilateral Authorship: a "me" or mentee focused	Purpose
Serves (adult) conventional goals	(Adult-Centric)	Focus: Minimally directive and/or highly relational	(Youth-Centric)	Serves playful (or youthful) goals
Adult-led spontaneous (nonrelational)	1. Preachy, pompous mentor driven, goal is vague. Mentor talks about whatever seems important at the time, mentee is disengaged (usually nonrelational)	2. Laissez-faire style Langhout, Rhodes, & Osborne, 2004) or acquaintance (Keller & Pryce, 2010). A relationship "about nothing," doing whatever both can agree on in the moment.	3. Jocular, overly playful (e.g., mentee has fun, play is spontaneous, but mentor feels insignificant, peripheral) and unstructured	Youth-led spontaneous (nonrelational)
Purpose	Unilateral Authorship: a "me" or mentor focused	Collaborative Authorship (collaboration)	Unilateral Authorship: a "me" or mentee focused	Purpose

Purpose	Unilateral Authorship: a "me" or mentor focused	Collaborative Authorship (collaboration)	Unilateral Authorship: a "me" or mentee focused	Purpose
Adult-oriented preventive and developmental activities or discussions (relational focus)	4. Role modeling or preventative Developmental focus on prevention (e.g., indirectly addresses conventional concerns (e.g., school, work); the focus is the mentee's (self-in-the-future) but in the context of close relationship	5. Developmental style (from Morrow & Styles, 1995) as both relational and collaborative; Includes talk about social interactions and fun, casual activities, "We" authorship via collaboration. Often later supports and encourages incorporation of goal-oriented interactions	6. Playmate as playful, supportive, relational interactions focused on youth's interests (e.g., may learn skills but indirectly; the focus is the mentee's self-in-the-present) within a close relationship	Youth-oriented preventive and developmental activities or discussions (relational focus)
Conventional skill development purpose More relevant to adult/societal goals, interests, or beliefs about what the mentee needs to prepare for future (Primarily goal-oriented focus)	7. Tutor (as in Keller & Pryce): Instrumental and conventional. Focused on developing skills for adult world, such as reading or writing) or goal-directed and future oriented (coaching of job skills). Often didactic.	8. Instrumental style (from Hamilton & Hamilton, 1992; 2005)) Collaborative, goal-oriented focus on character and competence; shared purpose in the goal they choose or agree to focus on; increasingly relational over time.	9. Teammate as instrumental and playful (e.g., older and wiser peer) helps teammate develop skills the mentee needs play well or may focus on the mentee's present concerns (e.g., peers)	Playful skill development Purpose more relevant to the youths' goals, interests, or emphasizes outcomes in the present (Primarily goal-oriented focus)
Remedial/ Intervention-oriented: Serves adults' goals (goal-oriented)	10. Prescriptive as heavy handed (often insensitive), bombastic, directed at problems an adult has identified	11. Apprenticeship style Highly instructive (directive), minimally relational but has some youth buy-in	12. Coach as active, fun, but very directive and minimally relational. Focus on youth's goals or skills	Remedial/ Intervention-oriented: Serves youths' goals (goal-oriented)
Purpose	Unilateral Authorship: a "me" or mentor focused	Collaborative Authorship (collaboration)	Unilateral Authorship: a "me" or mentee focused	Purpose

Hybrid roles

What appears more and more is that a hybrid role or relationship is essential. Morrow and Styles (1995) noted this when they suggested that in some ways, developmental relationships are only truly developmental relationships when they become more instrumental in nature.

Morrow and Styles wrote:

"After relatively extended and pacific periods primarily devoted to relationship-building—that is, to establishing trust and partnership, and enjoying activities—the majority of youth in developmental relationships began to demonstrate a pattern of independent help-seeking in which they voluntarily divulged such difficulties as poor grades or family strife … once their relationships were crystallized, nearly three-quarters of the developmental volunteers were successful in involving youth in conversations or activities that targeted such key areas of youth development as academic performance and classroom behavior" (1995 p. 20).

This hybrid approach—and the descriptions of the developmental and instrumental models—actually makes clear that the primary differences between developmental and instrumental styles are in whether the relationship starts off relational or goal-directed and to what extent the purpose of initial interactions is serious or playful. Over time, the developmental match (which starts off relational and playful) will become more goal- or problem-directed and more serious. Conversely, a good instrumental relationship will start out conventional and goal-directed but will later become more playful and relational. Successful mentoring relationships appear to include all four elements, plus one other essential element: They are all collaborative and youth-centered.

Conclusion

The goal of the CAMP Program Coordinator is to structure the program in such a way as to allow and support both approaches, and thereby fostering hybrid mentoring relationships that include the balance of goal directed and relational interactions best suited for each mentor and mentee pair. Through the use of developmental theories, mentors can be taught to provide sufficient empathy, praise and attention to become influential people in the lives of their mentors. This will allow them to foster their mentees' development as well as achieve their own developmental milestones.

CHAPTER 6. CAMP MENTORING MEETINGS AND PROGRAM PRACTICES

There are two main types of CAMP meetings that bring program participants together: the weekly afterschool meetings and the SuperSaturday events. These are the core activities that most CAMPs will choose to implement. Occasionally, CAMPs will conduct a Summer Program, discussed later in this chapter, which brings participants together a few times during the summer break for additional *CAMP Connectedness Curriculum* activities. While this is a great way to keep students engaged in the program, this element is optional.

Afterschool meetings

The heart and soul of a program is the weekly afterschool meetings that bring mentors and mentees together. Most programs begin meeting about a month into the school year, after enrolling mentees, notifying parents, and preparing mentors and Lead Mentors for their roles.

Once the meetings begin, matches meet every week of the school year, most often at the mentees' school. Some programs choose to have the younger students come to the mentors' high school—select the location that works best for you in terms of transportation and the quality and usefulness of the physical space. You may also choose to use both locations.

The meetings typically take place during traditional afterschool time, starting shortly after the end of classes and lasting about two hours. The school liaisons and Lead Mentors facilitate the arrival of all participants and help make sure everyone is ready for the activities to begin on time. A sample agenda appears below.

As shown in the sample agenda, most afterschool meetings are built around five main activities:

1. An icebreaker. This is a simple, playful activity designed to get the mentors and mentees moving, talking, and becoming engaged with the group. After a long day at school, many younger mentees will need to work out their restlessness. There is a growing body of evidence that interactive play and exercise produce neurochemical processes that enhance learning (Ratey & Hagerman, 2008). There are many resources for icebreaker activities, so find a selection that works well for your program and participants. (We have included some suggestions in the *CAMP Connectedness Curriculum*. Other resources include the *Encyclopedia of Icebreakers, Teamwork & Teamplay* (Cain & Jolliff, 1998), *Cowstails and Cobras* (Rohnke, 1989), and *New Games Book* (Flugelman, 1976). Remember the purpose here is not to teach anything, but rather to start the session on a fun note.

Sample CAMP Afterschool Meeting Agenda

Time	Activity
2:30–3:00 p.m.	Transportation to the meeting site
3:00–3:10	Icebreaker
3:10–3:20	3-2-1 Reflections (on life since the last meeting)
3:20–4:20	Listen and Learn Core Activity (with a snack included at some point)
4:20–4:30	3-2-1 Reflections (on the day)
4:30–pickup	Recreational time

2. 3-2-1 Reflections. In this activity, the mentor and mentee pair up and begin working together. Both share *three* good things that happened in their lives since their last meeting, *two* difficult or unfortunate things that happened, and *one* way they are trying to encourage more of those good experiences or prevent or address the negative ones. This sharing time usually takes about 10 minutes. The mentors do not counsel the mentees during this time. Rather, their role is to share their own reflections and listen to the mentee, providing encouragement and positive reinforcement for the good things the mentee brings up.

We feel that this time is absolutely critical to the success of the CAMP model. The 3-2-1 activity helps the mentor and mentee find their personal connection again before they start working together on the day's curriculum activity. It sets the stage for what comes after. This reflection time is also one of the main ways that the mentor provides the mentee with empathy, praise, and attention, three elements that are essential to the CAMP model. Mentors practice perspective taking here, as they listen and acknowledge the ups and downs of their mentees' world. Mentors also model supportive behavior and provide encouragement. The mentees benefit from having their thoughts and feelings validated and reflected back to them. The 3-2-1 Reflections activity facilitates the theory-based personal development that underpins the CAMP model.

By doing this reflection at the beginning of the session, mentors can identify any problems, issues, or distractions that might keep the youth from fully engaging in the day's activities. Lead Mentors and the school liaisons should be available during this time to provide support to any mentees who disclose a problem that needs attention.

3. Listen and Learn Core Activity. This is when the mentor and mentee work on the day's activity from the *CAMP Connectedness Curriculum*. These activities are focused on one of the connectedness "domains," such as school, family, or peers. Most activities have an initial task that the mentor and mentee work on together, followed by a collaborative period where they create something together for sharing with the larger group. The collaborative period may be an art project, a skit, a story, or some other creative product. The collaborative aspect of these activities helps facilitate perspective taking and teaches youth to defer immediate needs to a larger goal, a key developmental skill.

The sharing time at the end of collaboration is very important: It lets the pair take pride in what they accomplished together and allows other participants to learn how different pairs collaborated and found creative ways to express themselves. And, it's often the most enjoyable part of the day!

See Chapter 8 in this manual for further details on how these activities are sequenced. Remember that pressure to perform well during the core activity should be minimized; the emphasis should be on having fun. If program participants don't complete the more educational cooperative activities, that's OK. They should be encouraged to stay engaged in the curriculum. If mentees feel uncomfortable with an activity, they shouldn't be forced to participate.

4. Activity Reflections. At the end of the meeting, another form of reflection takes place in which mentors encourage mentees to reflect on the match. The same 3-2-1 framework is employed, but this time the focus is on the match and the day's activities: three things that went well, two things that did not, and one thing they can learn or do to accent the positive and reduce the negative. Mentors should encourage their mentees to be thoughtful about how the day went and help them articulate their feelings, especially when they talk about what did not go well, as this can be difficult for the young mentees. By doing this, the pair can work through any issues that came up in their relationship that day, while also providing the mentors with feedback about the activities that they can share with Lead Mentors and the Program Coordinator. You may want to build in a formal way of gathering this feedback periodically, such as asking mentors to write down the pair's observations and deposit them in a "Feedback Box" for the staff to review later.

5. A game or recreational time. Once the curriculum activity has ended, the group engages in open play or some recreational game until it's time to leave. Competitive games are motivating and energizing and should be included, but make sure that program participants don't get too caught up in "winning." The point of the mentoring program is to build relationships and self-esteem and aggressive competition can sometimes undermine these goals. Mentors and mentees who want to continue talking about an issue or working on a project during this time are encouraged to do so, but this open time is meant to wind down the day and send everyone home on a positive and fun note.

The role of Lead Mentors during afterschool meetings

Lead Mentors really take a "lead" role in facilitating these afterschool meetings. One of the big issues for peer support programs is a tendency to promote what is known as "deviancy training," a circumstance in which poorly supervised youth model negative behaviors and disrupt the activities and goals of the program. Even the most well-intentioned and best trained peer mentors can find themselves getting distracted by conversations with their peers—they are teenagers, after all. You want to avoid having the mentors model negative behavior or ignore their mentees while they "hang out" with their friends. This is where Lead Mentors come in.

Lead Mentors can lend support by:

- Taking attendance and getting participants organized at the beginning of the session
- Leading the icebreaker activity
- Introducing the curriculum activity and providing instructions
- Monitoring mentors and mentees to make sure that they are on task
- Providing support to any matches that are struggling to do an activity, having a personal issue, or are otherwise not engaged
- Facilitating the sharing of any collaborative projects
- Gathering feedback from mentors on how the day went
- Providing general supervision during the open play or recreational time

While Lead Mentors help ensure that matches are staying focused on the task at hand, they should also remember that CAMP requires a fun and supportive atmosphere. They should not be viewed by the participants as being a stern authority figure. Rather, they should present themselves as "mentors to the mentors"—someone who is there to help solve problems and give a gentle reminder if focus starts to wane. If a match is having a serious issue, or there are behaviors beyond a Lead Mentor's ability to address, the Program Coordinator and school liaisons can step in and help.

Other tips for afterschool meetings

The following recommendations address common issues for programs:

Deal with absenteeism. Since it is unlikely that all participants will make every meeting, figure out how you will handle times when some mentors or mentees are not present. Most CAMPs have the Lead Mentor step in and serve as a mentor for the day or double up one mentor or mentee with another pair. Just be sure that participants know what to expect when their partner is absent and never leave a mentor or mentee without someone to work with for the day. Even though CAMP is about one-to-one relationships, there is flexibility on a day-to-day basis.

Provide refreshments. Don't underestimate the importance of the snack. Youth need to eat more frequently than adults, and providing a light, healthy snack keeps up energy and breaks up the intense focus on curriculum activity in the middle of the session.

Shake things up. Take advantage of your physical space. If the matches have been meeting in the same room for several weeks, try to do a special session in the library or gymnasium. Provide occasional field trips to break the routine of the curriculum. Some CAMPs do this when the group finishes one of the curriculum "units," allowing for a transition between the major themes of the program and rewarding participants' hard work.

Plan around school breaks. Look at your schedule at the beginning of the year, note when many participants may be out because of holidays or other events, and plan your curriculum schedule accordingly. One difficult aspect of operating this type of school-based program is the logistical challenge presented by spring break, the long holiday season, and teacher in-service days. Make sure your afterschool meeting schedule has factored in all these gaps.

Develop activities that span several meetings. Offering activities that last over several sessions gives participants a sense of continuity. Both mentors and mentees will know what they're doing from one week to another and look forward to building on a project. (An example of one such multipart activity—the teacher interview—is described in Chapter 8.)

Integrate preexisting activities. Using activities from other curricula can be an effective way to develop a well-rounded program. However, it is important to compare the goals of other programs to CAMP's and make sure they align. To help clarify the connection between specific activities and the CAMP goals, Appendix B contains a list of activities that fall under each connectedness domain.

More information about afterschool meetings can be found in the *CAMP Connectedness Curriculum*.

SuperSaturdays

The SuperSaturday event is a primary culture-building aspect of the CAMP model. These events contribute to parent involvement and reinforce the positive peer culture fostered during the afterschool meetings. They also provide opportunities for having fun and exploring the community. Other attributes include:

- A chance for parents to see their child engaged in the mentoring relationship and to meet other parents whose children are involved in the program
- An opportunity for the Program Coordinator to connect with parents
- A way to involve community partners and other stakeholders
- Additional opportunities to conduct *CAMP Connectedness Curriculum* activities

SuperSaturdays are held every other month, beginning sometime within the first two months of the program. This allows most programs to offer a total of four SuperSaturdays during the school year. Most programs schedule the first event either shortly after matches are made, so that parents can meet their child's mentor/mentee, or prior to making matches, so participants get to know each other before being assigned a mentor/mentee. Some CAMPs even do the Meet-and-Greet matching activity (see page XX) during the initial SuperSaturday.

Planning SuperSaturday events. SuperSaturdays are typically held at the host school, the mentors' high school, or a community venue. Pick the location best-suited to the type of activity you've planned. Ideally, the events are attended not only by mentors, Lead Mentors, and mentees, but parents and families of participants, community members, and other stakeholders such as advisory committee members. Staff should include the Program Coordinator, school liaisons, principals, teachers, and other involved school personnel.

There are almost limitless possibilities for SuperSaturday programming. They can be built around field trips to cultural or natural attractions, service projects, community events, or recreational opportunities. Career explorations and high school orientations for middle school students are also popular choices.

Most CAMPs choose to do a half-day event structured around lunch. The day often follows a similar arc to one of the afterschool meetings: an icebreaker, "getting to know you" time, a curriculum activity, and a recreational game to end the day. See a sample schedule for a SuperSaturday below.

Most SuperSaturday activities are led by either the Program Coordinator, the school liaisons, or ideally the Lead Mentors. Putting the Lead Mentors in charge of the day gives them a great opportunity to show off their leadership skills in a group setting. You can also ask

Sample Agenda for a SuperSaturday Event

10:00–10:15 a.m. Icebreaker activity

10:15–10:30 Mentors and mentees do the 3-2-1 Reflection, parents socialize

10:30–11:30 Curriculum activity (parents and families participate as well)

11:30–12:30 p.m. Lunch

12:30–1:30 Game or recreational time

1:30–end Goodbyes and Q&A with the Program Coordinator

parents to volunteer to help lead some activities or serve as chaperones if the day is built around a field trip.

Tips for successful SuperSaturdays. In many ways SuperSaturdays provide the Program Coordinator with the most creative flexibility for nurturing program culture and shaping participants' experiences. Everything from a family hike in the woods to a curriculum activity on conflict resolution is in play. While this open approach offers many opportunities for innovation, it also means that these events will require more planning and preparation. In addition, it can be difficult to create continuity across these meetings; in fact, it's quite possible that no two SuperSaturday events will look quite the same.

Coordinators can build consistency into these events and maximize participant engagement by:

Providing frequent communication about the schedule of upcoming events. Outreach is critical for SuperSaturday attendance. Send multiple reminders to parents and ask Lead Mentors and school liaisons to remind students. Get permission slips in early if the event will involve an off-campus trip.

Offering transportation, child care for young siblings, or other services that make it easier for families to attend. Parents are a vital player in the SuperSaturday framework, so do everything you can to eliminate barriers to their participation.

Providing food and refreshments. Structuring the day around a meal provides an anchor to the event and creates a sense of community. Never discount the importance of food.

Engaging the parents at a meaningful level. SuperSaturdays are where the Program Coordinator reaches out to parents and solidifies their future involvement with the program. The coordinator *must* be visible and available on these days. He or she should answer parents' questions; ask for their feedback on improving the program; and discuss how their child is doing in CAMP and growing in fulfilling the mentor or mentee role. Principals, teachers, and other administrators can also help reach out to parents and make sure they are having fun and feeling positive about the event.

Involving families in all the day's activities. While parents will really enjoy watching their child interact with their mentor or mentee, they will also get a thrill out of participating in some of the types of activities the students do in CAMP. Select a few activities from the *CAMP Connectedness Curriculum* (or other sources) that you will *not* be doing during the afterschool meetings and save them for SuperSaturdays. Look for activities that involve cooperation and some kind of creative task.

Show parents what CAMP is all about so they can better understand how their child is benefiting from the program.

Try to end the annual SuperSaturday on a high note. A big group outing or special event can put a nice finishing touch on the year and leave youth and parents feeling good about the program (and perhaps considering participation during the next year). Remember that the Termination Ritual that happens at the end of each CAMP cycle can be difficult for the mentors and mentees. Ending with a special SuperSaturday event can reinforce the positive memories and lessons of the program.

CAMP summer program (optional)

Appendix A details an alternative version of the CAMP model known as the Distance Model. This model is a good fit for schools that are far apart, as it focuses on a more intensive daylong summer program schedule using the *CAMP Connectedness Curriculum,* supplemented by SuperSaturday events during the school year.

In addition to this formal model, there are many other creative ways that CAMPs can incorporate summer engagement into the traditional cross-campus framework. Keeping mentors and mentees involved, even a little bit, during the summer months can help facilitate multiyear participation and nurture mentoring relationships that pairs may want to renew in the fall.

Programs can keep participants engaged during the summer by:

- **Keeping the SuperSaturdays going.** If you can schedule two of these events in the summer, even if participation is down because of family vacations, it can help with recruitment in the fall. Even one event keeps the program fresh in families' minds.

- **Giving participants a summer project.** Look at the *CAMP Connectedness Curriculum* (or other sources) for ideas. Mentors and mentees may enjoy a fun summer project, such as growing a vegetable garden or documenting a family vacation. They can share their project at an early event the next year.

- **Communicating frequently.** At some point during the summer you will have your annual evaluation data and program feedback organized. Share what you have learned about the success and struggles of the program. Provide information about changes or plans for next year as soon as possible.

Other specific CAMP practices

While most of CAMP's developmental goals are facilitated through afterschool meetings, SuperSaturdays, and summer contact, a few additional program practices can help mentors and mentees move through their relationship in developmentally appropriate ways. Two practices, which govern the creation and dissolution of the mentoring match, give participants ownership over their relationship and mirror the cycle of healthy relationships that they will experience throughout their lives. We encourage all programs to implement the Meet and Great matching activity and the Match Termination Ritual within the framework provided here.

Meet-and-Greet matching activity

The Meet-and-Greet is done early in the program cycle, after mentors have gone through orientation and received their prematch training (see Chapter 7 for details). This activity can be done at a kick-off event that brings the mentors to the host school for the first time or it can be part of the first SuperSaturday event.

Programs have found that mentors and mentees are most satisfied with the program, at least initially, if they have a voice in the matches for their one-on-one relationship. Staff members also need to have some input in who gets matched together, but the goal of the Meet-and-Greet is to foster early enthusiasm for the program by facilitating some degree of mentor and mentee choice. The Meet-and-Greet is flexible enough to be done in as little as an hour or incorporated into a day's worth of activities (e.g., as part of a SuperSaturday).

The Meet-and-Greet activity itself is simple:

- Participants meet in groups of usually four or five mentees with the same number of mentors.
- They then engage in fun icebreakers or other group games. Be sure to select activities that involve a lot of group interaction and cooperation so that everyone mixes. You can scramble participants into new groups at the conclusion of each activity.
- Repeat the process until each mentor and mentee has had a chance to interact with each other during at least one activity.

The focus of these activities is deliberately not to quickly pair individual mentors and mentees, but to give everyone a chance to get to know each other in a group setting without any pressure. You want to avoid creating a process that will lead to conflict or disappointment.

At the end of the activity:

- Ask the mentees to provide the names of three mentors to whom they enjoyed talking. If the Meet-and-Greet has taken some time to complete, you may want to ask mentees to identify two mentors from the first half of the event and two from the last.
- Do not ask mentees who they would like to be matched with. Remember that this activity helps with matching; it is not a request service.
- Do not have the mentees rank the people they list. Asking for a first choice or ordering their list only creates expectations and potential disappointment.
- Also, ask the mentors to provide the names of the mentees they enjoyed interacting with. Since they will know the purpose of the activity is to ultimately facilitate pairing, they can provide names of specific mentees with whom they might be a good match.

Over the years, programs have found that the Meet-and-Greet process almost always results in mentees being matched with one of the three people they identified. By not ranking the names, they are simply happy to be matched with someone from their list. Start by looking for mentors and mentees who listed each other. Then go by mentee preference and use other information at your disposal, such as known common interests or similar family backgrounds, to match the remaining mentors and mentees. However, the Meet-and-Greet should allow the Program Coordinator to make "organic" matches that have already shown mutual interest and can hit the ground running in their new relationship.

The CAMP Match Termination Ritual

A structured end is critical to the CAMP model, for both prematurely ending relationships and matches that conclude as planned at the close of the program year. The Match Termination Ritual (Karcher, 2005a) is designed so program staff can systematically help the mentor and mentee reflect on their relationship and walk away with positive feelings and memories. It is specifically designed to help the mentee understand that the dissolution of the match is not because of his or her likability or worth. This is one of the main ways to ensure CAMPs "do no harm" to the students they serve.

Termination should provide closure and opportunities for learning for both participants. In order to do that, follow these steps when matches are terminated:

Identify and verbally clarify the reasons for termination with both the mentee and mentor. If the reasons involve the behavior of either party, this should be presented in a constructive manner. The person who engaged in the behavior (tardiness, rudeness, indifference, absenteeism, etc.) should be asked how that might make others feel, and the person who received the behavior could be asked how he or she might respond to such behavior in the future. This will serve as practice for the actual final meeting between the mentor and mentee.

Give the mentee and mentor the opportunity to discuss together what worked and didn't work in their relationship. Also, help them identify ways to handle future situations more effectively. The Program Coordinator should facilitate the conversation between the mentee and mentor in order to make sure that both parties express themselves positively and constructively. This information may be critical to successfully rematching the mentee or mentor (if that is an option).

Encourage both parties to share their feelings about ending their relationship. Mentors who are terminating because of time limitations or other reasons not related to the mentee need to make particularly clear to the mentee that he or she did not do anything to make the mentor leave. The mentor should share with the mentee the things about the mentee that he or she liked. Without appropriate sharing time, the mentee will feel unlovable or flawed in some way. The mentor should reassure the child that this is not the case.

Plan the next step. If the mentee is to be reassigned, discuss the new relationship with the mentee alone first. Help him or her identify mistakes that occurred with the previous mentor and discuss ways to avoid those mistakes in the future. (New behaviors may have been mentioned by the mentor in the mentor-mentee termination meeting.) If the match ended due to factors other than relationship conflict (e.g., a mentor's part-time job schedule changed), again reassure the mentee that he or she was not to blame and help him or her process any feelings about the termination of the relationship.

Arrange a meeting between the mentee and the new mentor. Set appropriate time boundaries (e.g., "We will meet weekly for one year and then see if we are able to spend more time together after that"). Establish guidelines for the relationship, especially if there were problems with the previous match. If a mentee has had significant problems with previous mentors, a trial period may be appropriate.

Even if the termination is planned as part of the end of the school year, give the mentee and mentor the opportunity to discuss what worked and didn't work in their relationship. Both parties should be encouraged to share their feelings about ending their relationship. If the relationship was very positive, help them identify things they learned about themselves. If the relationship was marked by some conflict, help them identify ways to handle future situations more effectively—just make sure they express themselves positively and constructively.

Reasons for termination. Recognize that prematurely terminating relationships may result from a variety of situations:

Match conflict. Sometimes it may become necessary to terminate a match due to conflicts between the mentee and mentor.

Exiting the program. Termination may also occur because either the mentee or the mentor leaves the program. The dropouts may occur as a result of relationship conflicts or other factors (e.g., a mentor's time limitations or a child leaving the school altogether).

Reassignment. It may become apparent that a mentee or mentor could work more effectively with another participant. In these cases, reassignment may be the best choice.

Often, termination will become public knowledge; it may be obvious to other program participants when a change has been made. The Program Coordinator and school liaisons should address this in the following ways in order to minimize incorrect assumptions and rumors:

If a mentee leaves the program for behavioral reasons. Explain to the others that you and the mentee have decided that this is not the best place for him or her to be at this time.

If a mentor leaves the program. Tell the others that he or she needed to leave the program. If the mentor's reasons for leaving were unrelated to the mentee, remind the other group members of this. If the reasons for leaving were related to the mentee, tell the group that you and the mentor decided that it would be best to find a mentor who had more in common with the mentee and would be better able to connect with him or her.

If mentees and mentors are reassigned, which should happen infrequently. Tell the group that everyone involved decided that it would be best to rearrange matches. Remind the others that sometimes after you get to know someone better, it becomes apparent that you may work more effectively with another person. If this happens, encourage mentees and mentors to approach the Program Coordinator to discuss reassignment.

Moving on

The practices described in this chapter all work together to form the relationship structure of CAMP:

- The Meet-and-Greet sets the stage by giving participants a voice in whom they are matched with and minimizes chances for disappointment
- Afterschool meetings provide opportunities for personal connection and collaboration
- SuperSaturdays frame the mentoring relationship in a culture of family and community support
- The Match Termination Ritual ensures that all match closures are handled in an appropriate manner that lets the participants retain the positive gains they made in the program

By using this framework, CAMPs position their participants for meaningful interactions and relationships within the developmental philosophy of the program. The following chapters explain how the training participants receive—and the *CAMP Connectedness Curriculum* itself—support the relationship framework.

CHAPTER 7. MENTOR TRAINING AND SUPERVISION

Proper training and preparation of mentors is critical to the success of all mentoring programs. Peer mentoring programs, such as CAMP, face an even greater need to prepare mentors for their role: The older youth serving as mentors often have fewer communication and relationship skills than adult mentors, and they certainly have less life experience to draw on when helping mentees solve problems. If your CAMP is going to build strong mentoring relationships, participant training is where it begins.

Most of the information, materials, and guidelines for training CAMP mentors can be found in the *CAMP Mentor Training Guide*, one of the companion resources to this manual. The *Training Guide* covers the full spectrum of prematch and ongoing training that mentors receive during the course of the year. Initially, a full-day or two half-day training event should be conducted to orient the mentors to the program, followed by ongoing training on at least a monthly basis. However, we've provided a summary of the training below.

Prematch mentor training

Prematch training can boost mentors' self-confidence and help them believe they can be successful in this role. There are several other goals for prematch training as well:

1. Clarify their roles and responsibilities
2. Explain who the mentees will be and what their interactions will look like
3. Develop communication and problem-solving skills they can use in their matches and which they will model for their mentees
4. Teach perspective-taking skills that allow them to provide empathy, praise, and attention to the mentee
5. Provide an overview of the curriculum and how it will be used throughout the year
6. Practice the mentoring role, often through role-play activities

Prematch mentor training follows the orientation session and takes place early in the year after the final pool of mentors has been set. Be sure to complete this training before mentors meet with their mentees. They need to have the skills, understanding, and confidence to get that first meeting off on the right foot.

Topics covered during prematch training include:

- The role and responsibilities of the mentor
- How mentors can help mentees
- How to handle problems if they arise
- Staff roles in supporting the mentors
- Mentors' hopes and concerns
- Review of the schedule for the year
- Logistics, such as transportation to the host school and getting permission for off-campus activities

Remember that this initial training is designed to provide mentors with the information and confidence they need to get the match *started*. Trying to cover too much ground during the prematch training (especially some of the more complicated developmental theory) can leave mentors confused and oversaturated with information. That's why CAMP provides several opportunities for ongoing training throughout the year, as described below.

The *CAMP Mentor Training Guide* provides further detail and instruction about prematch mentor training. Prematch training is a good time to provide each mentor with a handbook. This is typically a three-ring binder that mentors can use for training handouts, curriculum worksheets, and other program materials. The handbooks can be used during trainings throughout the year and provide mentors with a lasting record of what they have learned in the program. A sample table of contents for a mentor handbook appears in the *CAMP Mentor Training Guide*.

Ongoing mentor training

CAMP mentors receive several trainings throughout the year that reinforce concepts learned during prematch training and provide new skills that will be useful as their match progresses. While ongoing training is not aligned directly with specific *CAMP Connectedness Curriculum* modules, it is designed so that it follows the natural course of the relationship. There is greater emphasis on building connections and providing support early in the year; later training focuses on relationship-strengthening strategies; and the final sessions relate to saying goodbye and wrapping up the relationship at the end of the year.

Ongoing mentor training is typically done through four large-group presentations, outlined below. Program Coordinators have flexibility in when they offer these, but we have found that scheduling the first training about a month into the match and the last about a month before the end of the year tends to work well. The other two sessions can be scheduled in between, at participants' convenience. Most programs conduct these sessions as an add-on to a SuperSaturday.

Supporting CAMP matches

In addition to prematch and ongoing training, peer mentors need plenty of other support as they move through the program year. Chances are that even the best mentors will have times when they are frustrated, unsure about how to solve a problem, or feel dissatisfied with the program. If your CAMP is going to produce strong relationships and positive impacts, you must be prepared to offer a variety of supports.

Supervising matches. Supporting participants begins with the supervision they receive during afterschool meetings. This is where Lead Mentors must shine. The Lead Mentors should be engaged with participants and help support the matches by:

Ongoing CAMP Mentor Trainings

1. Building Connectedness Through Empathy, Praise, and Attention

- Conflict resolution styles
- Being a good listener
- Effective praise
- Positive reinforcement
- Defining who you are (using the Hemingway Measure and Social Interest Scales)
- Brainstorming connectedness activities

2. Theoretically Evolving Activities in Mentoring (TEAM) Framework

- The TEAM framework
- Trusting others
- Constructive criticism
- Solution-focused helping
- Motivating struggling students
- Behavior types and how to handle them

3. Perspective Taking

- Introduction to the perspective-taking developmental model
- Assertiveness
- Promoting social skills
- Finding alternatives
- Problem-solving steps

4. Hello and Goodbye

- Welcoming someone new
- Saying goodbye

Being available and visible. Lead Mentors should walk around the room as participants work on curriculum activities and be available to answer any questions.

Looking for matches that may be struggling. Signs of a problem include minimal conversation between the mentor and mentee; expressions of disinterest or arguing; only one of the pair doing the activity; and participants talking with friends or engaging in other disruptive behavior. Lead Mentors should provide support and help the pair work through any issues, bringing in the school liaison as needed to provide additional guidance.

Reminding participants to stay on task. Lead Mentors should make sure that all mentors and mentees are focused on what they are supposed to be doing, reminding them that there are opportunities for open play and conversation built into the schedule of the day. They should not let one mentor or mentee create problems for the rest of the group.

Reporting concerns or problems to the school liaisons and the Program Coordinator. Because of their direct interaction with the mentors and mentees, Lead Mentors are likely to have more inside information about how things are going than the adults in the program. Encourage them to share their observations, even if they are negative.

School liaisons and the Program Coordinator should also observe matches and provide support during meeting time. That's when participants can become dissatisfied with the program and relationships can go sour. So, recognize that match support begins literally while the match is meeting.

Checking in with participants. In addition to providing support during meetings, the Program Coordinator should check in with mentors, mentees, and parents periodically. Contact parents of mentors and mentees at least monthly during the early part of the year. This can be done in person at the SuperSaturday events or during parent-teacher conferences or through phone calls or e-mails. Ask parents how they think the match is going and see if they have questions, concerns, or suggestions.

For mentors and mentees, check-in times are built into the *CAMP Connectedness Curriculum*. These are known as relationship reflection activities that take place at four points during the year, often at the end of a curriculum "unit" and before the Termination Ritual. These relationship reflections provide mentors and mentees with an opportunity to think about how their relationship is going, what they can do to improve it, and what program changes may be needed to facilitate stronger relationships. The relationship reflections are a great way to get mentors to internalize what they are learning about themselves through the program, while also providing valuable information that can help solve issues for individual matches or the program as a whole.

You may also want to check in with teachers, counselors, and other school staff who interact with your mentors and mentees. Consider conducting a survey to find out: What changes are they seeing in the young person? Have they heard any positive or negative feedback about the program or the mentoring relationship? Collect as much feedback as you can—from different sources—about how participants are feeling during the course of the year.

Participant recognition

One of the best ways to encourage participants and help them commit to the program is to frequently recognize their efforts. You don't have to provide fancy or expensive gestures. Rather, you can make mentors and mentees feel good about their participation by:

- Highlighting the great work they have been doing in a program newsletter or in the school paper
- Creating a "match of the week" that is singled out for special recognition
- Giving mentors and Lead Mentors occasional "thank you" cards or small gift cards
- Throwing a pizza or ice cream party to celebrate the end of a curriculum section

- Telling parents about the growth you have seen in their child and encouraging parents to praise participants for their hard work as well
- Ending the year with a special SuperSaturday or other event

Remember that your participants work very hard to make the program successful. They stretch themselves personally and take chances learning and practicing new skills. Make sure they know just how much you appreciate their efforts.

CHAPTER 8. THE CAMP CONNECTEDNESS CURRICULUM

The heart of the CAMP model is the *CAMP Connectedness Curriculum* that guides the match activities during the afterschool meetings and, to a lesser degree, during SuperSaturdays. The curriculum is tied to six core "domains":

- Connectedness to self
- Connectedness to teachers
- Connectedness to friends
- Connectedness to peers (classmates)
- Connectedness to reading
- Connectedness to culture

Your program is not limited to working in these six domains. Other CAMPs have included units on connectedness to religion, community, and the future (e.g., goal setting and planning for the future). However, the domains listed above align with the *CAMP Connectedness Curriculum.*

Programs are also free to develop their own activities or incorporate those from other sources that can help build connectedness in mentors and mentees. In fact, programs are encouraged to adapt and adjust the curriculum over time to tailor activities to the unique needs of their students and school and to keep the program from becoming boring or repetitive for multiyear participants.

When assembling your curriculum, there are a few important points to keep in mind:

Building bonds is foremost. Whatever activities the mentor/mentee pairs engage in, the activity is less important than the emotional bond that is formed between the participants during this time. To facilitate that, the program must define a clear, consistent structure to keep mentors and mentees engaged and focused on their relationship.

Activities should be fun yet thought provoking. The key to a successful curriculum is having activities that are fun, low key, and nonprescriptive. At the same time, they should encourage thought and discussion about interpersonal relationships and the individual's (and the family's) place in the larger society.

Curriculum activities should build a base of shared experience. Whatever you plan, the activity should help the mentor/mentee pairs communicate more effectively and develop perspective-taking skills within their relationship. For example, computer games typically shift the focus away from the match, while reading aloud remains interactive and provides opportunities to comment on how a story or character reflects one's own life experience.

Activities should focus on self-awareness and social understanding. The curriculum should encourage social skills such as cooperation, empathy, assertiveness, and caring in addition to perspective taking. At the same time, the curriculum should focus on affective or physical engagement with others, the larger society, or one's own self.

Core activities

In this chapter we discuss some core activities related to the six domains. These examples should form a large part of your curriculum and should also serve as the model for any new curricula. In the *CAMP Connectedness Curriculum* are several ready-to-use activities; explanations for why they are useful for developing connectedness, perspective taking, and social skills; and instructions for how to create theoretically consistent activities for subsequent years of program operations or that address local needs.

Connectedness to self, teachers, and friends (fall term)

Controlling Your Anger. The first set of activities centers on anger management. The activities promote self-awareness by exploring the triggers for anger and identifying feelings that often precede anger. They address connectedness to others by making mentees aware of the various ways anger can be expressed and things that make others angry. The activities help mentees develop social skills by exploring positive ways to express anger and to mitigate outbursts by creating mental and physical space.

The activities promote perspective taking by helping mentees recognize negative emotions as they're happening. And, they allow mentors to provide emotional support through empathy, praise, and attention.

Getting To Know Your Teachers. The second set of activities, spanning four afterschool meetings, promotes connectedness to teachers by asking each mentee to plan and conduct an interview with one of the teachers at their school. The process of getting to know a teacher on a personal level also builds empathy and perspective-sharing skills. The interview is completed during the second meeting, so there is ample time to reflect on the interview and the student/teacher relationship during the next two meetings.

Mentees are encouraged to think about how the teacher they interviewed is similar to or different from themselves. By sharing their reflections, mentees generate group discussion about relationships between students and teachers.

What's Important in a Friend? The final curricular activity in the fall spans three afterschool meetings. During these exercises, the group explores what qualities are important in a friend and different ways to communicate with friends. Reflections on what we value in friends and the meaning of friendship help mentees consider the quality of their own friendships. These sessions pave the way for further discussion of communication styles in the spring, including the differences among passive, aggressive, and assertive communications.

Connectedness to reading (winter term). This sequenced set of reading activities lasts from the beginning of the winter term almost until spring break. First, the pair takes a trip to the library to select and read books, which they then rewrite. Subsequent sessions teach the mentors and mentees a model of social development to apply to the characters in the books and use animals to explore different levels of perspective taking. Finally, the matches team up with other pairs to act out their new stories and guess which levels and styles of development are depicted.

Connectedness to classmates (spring term). The final set of core activities focuses on getting along with classmates, as distinct from friends. This curriculum emphasizes negotiation and communication strategies that would be especially helpful in dealing with peers, such as labels, stereotypes, conflict resolution, and nonverbal communication.

Reflecting on these topics and developing these skills helps mentees learn to deal with peers in a more respectful and diplomatic way. These skills should help them make a more positive contribution to the peer culture at their school, as well as set the stage for the Termination Ritual at the end of the school year.

Connectedness to culture (throughout the year and during summer). As previously discussed, these activities are primarily accomplished through SuperSaturdays and the optional summer session. Field trips off campus—whether a hike through a nature preserve, a picnic in the park, a visit to a museum, or a volunteer experience at a local food bank—can help connect youth to their community. This bond is strengthened by having family and community members join in the activities.

Sequencing the curriculum during the year

While there is no right or wrong way to schedule the curriculum, we strongly recommend that programs start with the activities related to connectedness to self. These activities are designed to explain important concepts at the beginning of the program, get participants to explore the idea of connectedness, and provide opportunities for self-reflection heading into the match.

Once the initial self-connectedness activities are completed, programs have discretion in how they sequence other activities. In the examples above, we propose focusing on connectedness to teachers to try to build positive school perceptions early in the year. However, some programs ease into things by starting with connectedness to reading so that mentors and mentees can explore literature together as a way of bonding. Many CAMPs have found that connectedness to culture is a good section for the end of the year or the summer, as it relates to participants' home life and larger community.

When scheduling the curriculum during the course of the year, be sure to allow for holidays and other school breaks. Also leave room for the relationship reflections described in Chapter 7, which supplement the core meeting activities, and newly matched games. You may also need to schedule around mentor trainings and other program and school events.

Below is a sample of what the full school-year schedule might look like for a typical program, including holidays that might impact the schedule. Adjust this schedule to align with the school year in your district.

Month	Curriculum Event/Connectedness Domain	Holidays & Breaks
September	Mentor Orientation/Training	Labor Day
	Mentor Self-Reflection: Connectedness	
	Mentee Orientation	
	Meet-and-Greet Event	
	Discuss Connectedness Profiles	
October	Self, Day 1: What Makes Me Angry?	Columbus Day
	Self, Day 2: When I'm Angry …	Halloween
	Self, Day 3: Avoiding Getting Angry	
	Newly Matched Game Practice #1	
November	Teachers, Day 1: Overview (Planning)	Veterans Day
	Teachers, Day 2: Conducting Interview	Thanksgiving
	Teachers, Day 3: Presenting	
	Teachers, Day 4: Reflecting	

December	Newly Matched Game Practice #2	Winter Break
	Friends, Day 1: Different Opinions	
	Friends, Day 2: What's Important	
	Friends, Day 3: Disagreeing w/Friends	
January	(Catch-Up Day: Flexible/Open)	Winter Break
	Relationship Reflection #1	MLK Day
	Newly Matched Tournament I	
February	Reading, Day 1: Visit the Library	Presidents' Day
	Reading, Day 2: Reading Together	
	Reading, Day 3: Zero, One, Two, We	
March	Relationship Reflection #2	Spring Break
	Reading, Day 4: Fight/Flight Strategies	
	Reading, Day 5: Yumewii Mountain	
	Reading, Day 6: Being an Animal	
April	Newly Matched Game Practice #3	
	Reading, Day 7: Writing Skits	
	Reading, Day 8: Practicing Skits	
	Reading, Day 9: SHOWTIME	
May	Newly Matched Game Practice #4, After Relationship Reflection #3	Memorial Day
	Peers, Day 1: Perspective Taking	
	Peers, Day 2: Communicating	
	Peers Day 3: Problem Solving	
June (before school ends)	Newly Matched Tournament	
	Match Termination Ritual (Closure Event)	
July–August	Summer CAMP (Optional)	

Fidelity in program implementation

Implementing the curriculum with fidelity (i.e., as planned or intended) conveys a vision, a set of values, and principles that undergird the program and the mentoring relationship. One common factor that makes interventions effective is the degree to which program staff is committed to an approach and adheres to a common understanding of what a participant is likely to gain from the program (Wampold, 2001). When it is unclear what the program "is about," it is less likely to have a lasting impact.

CHAPTER 9. EVALUATING PROGRAMS

Evaluating the program: Assessing fidelity of implementation and measuring outcomes

The ongoing evaluation of your program is essential. The *outcome evaluation* may be necessary to document the impact of your CAMP, and this evidence may be very helpful when negotiating with administrators (for resources, space, or continuation) or funders, who want evidence of impact (Karcher, 2005c).

The *formative evaluation,* however, is much more critical to program improvement efforts. To honor the mission statement of the program shared at the start of the manual, you must not only measure the effects of the program on both mentors and mentees, but also make concerted efforts to ensure that the program is implemented with fidelity, as planned and described in the manual. Appendix 9A lists many of these key elements to consider.

Even if the program is found to have a positive effect for the mentors and mentees as a whole, some youth may fare poorly and often only a careful evaluation can reveal this. For example, in one evaluation of CAMP (Karcher, 2005b), CAMP was found to have a positive effect overall on key program outcomes (viz. school connectedness, self-esteem, and social skills); but it also was discovered that the mentors varied in their attendance rates. Those mentees meeting with mentors who attended less consistently got worse and reported declines in self-esteem, particularly in physical self-esteem.

Just because a program can demonstrate an impact does not mean that it could not be improved. This requires other types of evaluation which fall under the umbrella term, formative evaluation. We differentiate two types: implementation and process approaches to formative evaluation. The implementation evaluation has to do with making sure your program is working the way you expect it to. The process evaluation tests to see that the processes by which you think your program has its effects on outcomes are taking place.

Unique selling point for CAMP: Program-specific outcome measurements

The program is unique in that it was developed and tested alongside a parallel process of development and testing the measures used to assess change resulting from CAMP. More specifically, CAMP was designed to effect connectedness, and the *Hemingway Measure of Adolescent Connectedness* was designed to assess change on these psychological constructs. Both the program and the measure have undergone considerable field testing. One of the main benefits of using the CAMP approach (including the mentoring training and program curriculum designed to foster connectedness) is that the outcome measures used to measure impact are intimately tied to the program content.

In addition, prior research reveals which domains of connectedness change as a result of participation in CAMP (for mentors and mentees), and these are the outcomes included in the evaluation described in this chapter. We present the measures used to assess program impact, both on connectedness as well as on self-esteem. We review the scales, what they measure, how they are scored, and other information necessary for the effective use of these scales in program operations and evaluation.

Therefore, of the two types of evaluation you should consider undertaking—a formative evaluation and outcome evaluation—the formative evaluation provides the starting place for a comprehensive evaluation plan as well as a program improvement plan.

The outcome evaluation can't take place until the formative evaluation demonstrates satisfactory program operations. The use of both approaches, in this order, is essential to building, maintaining, and demonstrating a strong program.

Two types of formative evaluations

The outcome evaluation should only be undertaken once your formative evaluation reveals a high level of program fidelity. Program fidelity reflects the degree to which the program is implemented as prescribed in the manual and as intended by you on the ground (i.e., following any programmatic changes made to accommodate the needs of your school or participating youth). So the formative evaluation is what you should undertake for the first year of the program (and every year thereafter), and only after a high fidelity program has been established should the outcome evaluation be undertaken.

Formative evaluation: Beginning with implementation

In the formative evaluation, you want to make sure that all program elements are in place and working correctly. For example, as part of the formative evaluation we assess whether mentors showed up consistently because that is an important program activity. Other key program elements include the activities of recruitment, training, matching, and operating the program. All of these are elements, when you implement them more fully and effectively—that is, with greater fidelity— yield bigger program impacts. As a few examples, you achieve a high degree of fidelity in regard to program *implementation* when you have evidence that:

- You recruited mentors with high scores on "attitudes towards youth" and "social interest" and you have a balance of mentees that includes youth at low, medium, and higher risk for academic and social difficulties

- The program has been delivered consistently

- Participants have been able to consistently get through all of the elements of the meeting period (climbed the developmental ladder each meeting—from icebreakers, touching base time, learning activity, and collaboration) and progressed through all of the curriculum you planned to cover in the year

- SuperSaturday events were held and achieved a high level of parental participation (e.g., >75%)

- Ninety percent of matches were sustained over the academic year

- The summer program was held and you reached your anticipated goal for attendance

How do you conduct the formative evaluation? The first step should be to document the presence of each activity or program element as part of the *implementation evaluation*. The second step is to attempt to measure the proximal "outcomes" of these activities using a *process evaluation*. There are some elements of the implementation evaluation (did it happen) that are tied to the process evaluation (did it work). For example, for each of the examples below, the first part is about implementation; the second part is about whether what happened had its intended effect (whether the changes took place).

1. You used attendance sheets to note how many mentors and mentees participated in pretraining and how many mentors attended postmatch trainings (implemented training), but do you have evidence that mentors have learned the material (i.e., that learning occurred)?

2. You documented that matches were made, and were made using information from the Meet-and-Greet, but did you determine an adequate degree of match satisfaction at the start of the year and did you check that the matches reflected an adequate degree of relationship quality at midyear (per mentor and mentee reflections on the match)?

Process Evaluation

When it comes to assessing the experience of the mentors and mentees to ensure the program is operating properly, there is a fine line between a formative and process evaluation. The process evaluation is particularly important in peer programs where the intended positive effects of peer interactions can go awry and have unanticipated negative effects.

The process evaluation attempts to measure the presence of the program's "mechanism of change." The variables that explain the way in which the program activities effect program outcomes are the *mediators*—they capture how the effect of the program is "explained" (or occurs as a function of) specific program activities. In CAMP, we have program activities (curriculum, a matching process, closing activity, and SuperSaturdays) which we created in order to cause these particular mediating processes that we think account for the positive changes CAMP can affect. These activities are intended to facilitate connectedness, assure compatibility of matches, ensure satisfactory match closure, and foster parents' positive experiences of involvement in the process.

We only know if our program components result in these mediating intrapersonal processes if we measure them. For example, you should conduct a midyear evaluation of the mentoring relationship. We assume the activities that comprise the program will foster strong matches, but we don't know if this intermediary or mediating process (creation of strong matches) has taken place until we measure it and correlate the presence of these program processes and youths' outcomes. We also would rather learn at midyear (than after the program is over) that these processes are working or not.

Midyear evaluation of mediating processes: Three surveys

As part of a process evaluation we measure self-reported match quality and satisfaction at midyear. We assess the experience of relationship quality and trust that is believed to result from mentors' consistency with a survey that yields numerical scores representing the degree of relationship quality and trust reported by mentees.

There are several ways in which process evaluation questions can be addressed with correlations between process measures of implementation fidelity and outcome assessments. We can correlate our measures of program fidelity, such as attendance (program activity), with relationship quality (psychological and interpersonal process) to see if they are related—that is, to see if variation in attendance is related to relationship quality at midyear. If so, then we need to (a) reduce variation in attendance and (b) do so by fostering higher attendance if we find higher attendance is correlated with higher relationship satisfaction. The schedule of which surveys to administer at which point is provided in Appendix 9e. and 9f.

Feedback loop—participant satisfaction (i.e., subjective assessments of the salience of program elements). Evaluating whether or not the program elements were received or experienced as intended tells us if they hit their mark, "caused," or created in the participants the experience we intended. We ask specific questions to see if program activities were salient:

- Did those who were trained feel they were adequately trained?
- Did those who used the connectedness curriculum find it useful, engaging, and relevant?
- Does increased training correlate with higher levels of mentor efficacy?

You want to know answers to these questions as soon as possible so you can intervene, get information from youth about how to improve the program, and then implement those changes as you go along. You don't want to discover this information at the end of the year that even though you trained mentors and mentees, they did not feel trained or remained confused about the goals of the program all year long. Better to assess and ensure along the way that elements are "going right."

We also collect data at midyear and at the start of the program to assess with surveys a number of indicators of the program's salience or influence on the youth involved. These surveys are listed in Appendix F.

Evaluating the effect of training on mentor efficacy

The evaluation of training likely entails both implementation and process evaluation efforts. As part of the implementation evaluation, you will take attendance, observe training to ensure youth participated (were engaged), and note whether the training is implemented fully and without any hitch. Then, we estimate whether training has increased mentors' subsequent feeling of mentor self-efficacy (the process evaluation of mentor training). We also ask the mentors to report on what they learned and whether they feel trained. These questions provide qualitative responses to the question: Were mentors satisfied with the training and did they feel like it fostered their efficacy as mentors?

Mentor Self-Efficacy Scale (DuBois). The Mentor Self-Efficacy Scale is provided at intake and again after training (which allows us to measure changes in self-reported Mentor Self-Efficacy Scale scores from intake to posttraining). It provides an indication of how confident each mentor is in her ability to perform various mentoring functions. This comparison of the mentors' self-efficacy scores after training to scores before training should provide a quantitative measure of the impact of training. It also can reveal which mentors may need additional training or support from Lead Mentors.

Program and Mentor Connectedness Scales (Karcher). To assess the salience or impact of the mentoring for mentees, we use the *Mentee Connection Scales* provided to mentees at midyear. There are two of these. The *Program Connection Scale* tells us how the youth feels about the program and its activities, while the *Mentor Connection Scale* tells us how the mentee feels about the mentor. Mentor's assessments of the utility of the activities can be obtained using the Activity Reflection cards collected at the end of each meeting.

Mentee Relationship Quality Scales. Mentees also complete scales that reveal how "listened to" and motivated they felt by their mentor (scales by DuBois & Hirsch, 1990). Another scale even assesses the presence of negative experiences (e.g., being teased) and another reveals how much the mentee feels like he or she is the focus of the mentor's attention (how "youth-centered" the mentor is)(scales by Grossman & Johnson, 1999) and another about how much the mentor helped with growth and personal goals (DuBois, 2012) .

Evaluation based on the program logic model

Most funders will request or appreciate seeing your logic model, and the entire program evaluation should be based on the logic model. As described above, the first type of evaluation program coordinators must conduct is an evaluation of whether the program was actually implemented as intended and then whether the processes that were supposed to occur (illustrated in the logic model) took place. We need a visual illustration of what this looks like to summarize for funders, evaluators, and other stakeholders how CAMP works. One example of a logic model for a CAMP is presented in Figure 5.

We describe program fidelity in terms of the program's logic model. To convey what program activities should occur (and why) we present them in this logic model. There are several ways to draft a logic model. This one is consistent with the U.S. Office of Juvenile Justice and Delinquency Prevention (OJJDP), which has traditionally and recently provided considerable funding for youth mentoring. We chose this model so that if you decide to adapt it for a grant proposal, you have the format requested by at least one funding agency.

In this model, you see the rationale for the program in terms of a general problem, youth disconnection. We note some of the consequences to society and to the youth themselves of our not addressing this problem—these consequences become the program outcomes we describe later in the chapter. The problem informs the goals: to implement CAMP and circumvent these deleterious consequences.

Under subproblems, we provide further rationale or justification of the need to actively structure developmental experiences like CAMP to address the problem. This sets the stage for the program objectives, which are listed below the subproblems. Notice, without the subproblems statement, it is not necessarily clear why specific program structures (e.g., activities, training, supervision) are so critical (viz. to avoid deviancy effects resulting from poorly structured or naturally occurring peer interactions).

The objectives inform the activities of the program. "We set out do to Y (objectives) and do it by providing X (activities)." These activities are organized in terms of a framework described by Durlak and DuPre (2008), who emphasize the following elements of programs:

- Program component fidelity
- Program dosage (duration and intensity of program participation)
- Quality of program delivery
- Responsiveness of participants to the program
- Adaptability of the program to constituent needs
- Appropriateness of the program's reach (those it serves)

We've broken down key elements of program implementation for CAMP under these categories, and they are presented in Appendices C and E. We illustrate these later when we give examples of high- and low-fidelity programming. We use each of these program activities to create our checklist to assess fidelity, and reveal the specific interpersonal or psychological process resulting from the activity that is believed to make mentoring work.

These processes are listed under Output Measures. In the formative evaluation, first we assess whether the program activity was present (implementation evaluation) and then whether it elicited the interpersonal or psychological process is was supposed to (process evaluation). Once we are sure the activities are all taking place, and they are working as intended, then we can shift to the outcomes evaluation.

Both types of formative evaluations (implementation and process evaluations) can be summarized using the logic model. The implementation type of formative evaluation, which is essential to evaluating whether or not the program was implemented with fidelity, is shown in the middle of the logic model. It illustrates the parts of the program that you planned to provide to youth (and which we indicate are essential to creating a bona fide program). The list of program activities can be used to ask questions such as, "Did you have the space you expected, did kids show up, were there activities to engage in, and were other supervisory supports in place to foster the mentoring interactions?"

If the answer to each of these implementation questions is yes, you have a high fidelity program. If it is no, you have a low fidelity program. If you have a low fidelity program, and your outcome

Figure 5. Logic Model for Cross-Age Mentoring Program

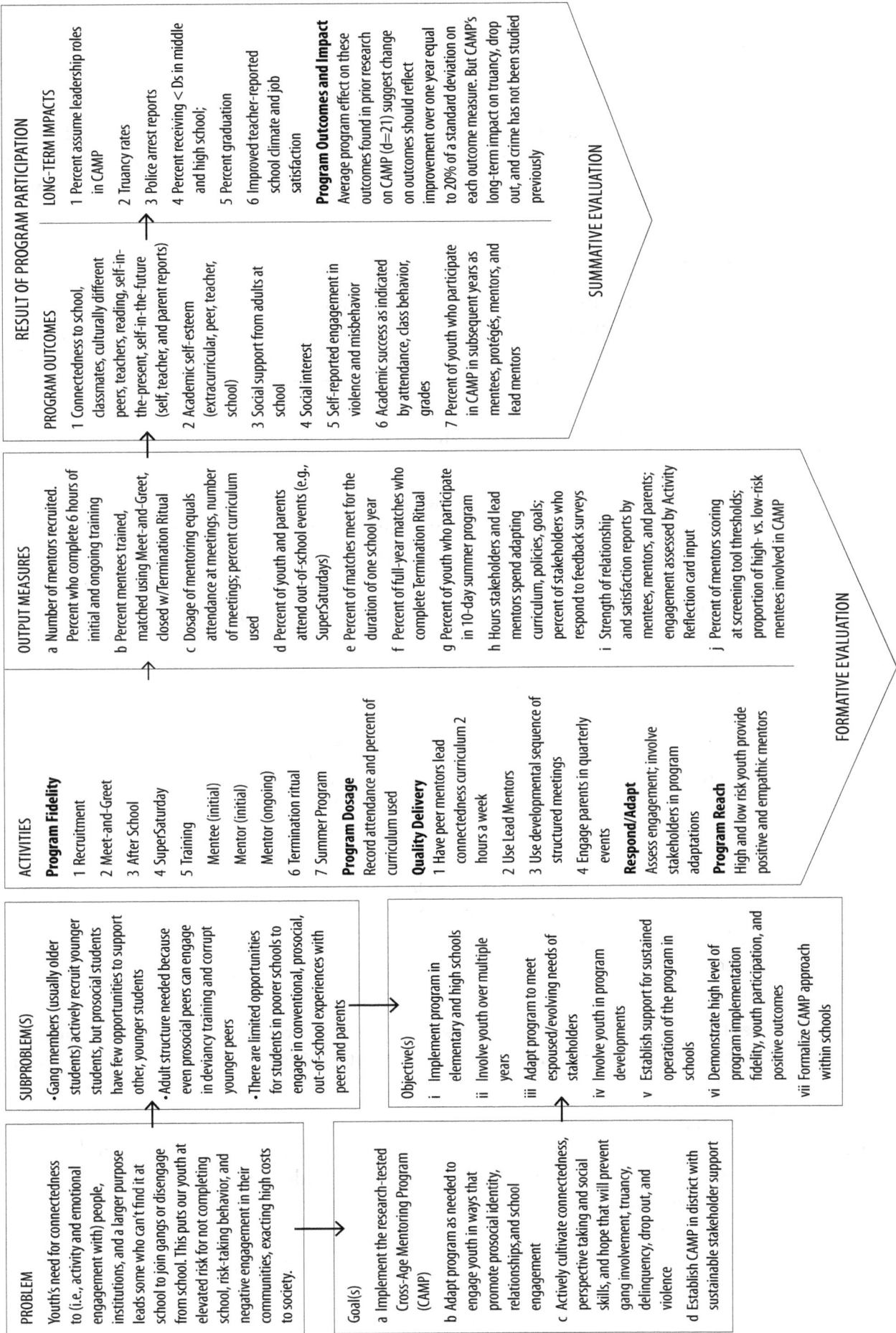

PROBLEM

Youth's need for connectedness to (i.e., activity and emotional engagement with) people, institutions, and a larger purpose leads some who can't find it at school to join gangs or disengage from school. This puts our youth at elevated risk for not completing school, risk-taking behavior, and negative engagement in their communities, exacting high costs to society.

Goal(s)

a Implement the research-tested Cross-Age Mentoring Program (CAMP)

b Adapt program as needed to engage youth in ways that promote prosocial identity, relationships, and school engagement

c Actively cultivate connectedness, perspective taking and social skills, and hope that will prevent gang involvement, truancy, delinquency, drop out, and violence

d Establish CAMP in district with sustainable stakeholder support

SUBPROBLEM(S)

• Gang members (usually older students) actively recruit younger students, but prosocial students have few opportunities to support other, younger students

• Adult structure needed because even prosocial peers can engage in deviancy training and corrupt younger peers

• There are limited opportunities for students in poorer schools to engage in conventional, prosocial, out-of-school experiences with peers and parents

Objective(s)

i Implement program in elementary and high schools

ii Involve youth over multiple years

iii Adapt program to meet espoused/evolving needs of stakeholders

iv Involve youth in program developments

v Establish support for sustained operation of the program in schools

vi Demonstrate high level of program implementation fidelity, youth participation, and positive outcomes

vii Formalize CAMP approach within schools

ACTIVITIES

Program Fidelity

1 Recruitment
2 Meet-and-Greet
3 After School
4 SuperSaturday
5 Training
   Mentee (initial)
   Mentor (initial)
   Mentor (ongoing)
6 Termination ritual
7 Summer Program

Program Dosage

Record attendance and percent of curriculum used

Quality Delivery

1 Have peer mentors lead connectedness curriculum 2 hours a week
2 Use Lead Mentors
3 Use developmental sequence of structured meetings
4 Engage parents in quarterly events

Respond/Adapt

Assess engagement; involve stakeholders in program adaptations

Program Reach

High and low risk youth provide positive and empathic mentors

OUTPUT MEASURES

a Number of mentors recruited. Percent who complete 6 hours of initial and ongoing training

b Percent mentees trained, matched using Meet-and-Greet closed w/Termination Ritual

c Dosage of mentoring equals attendance at meetings, number of meetings; percent curriculum used

d Percent of youth and parents attend out-of-school events (e.g., SuperSaturdays)

e Percent of matches meet for the duration of one school year

f Percent of full-year matches who complete Termination Ritual

g Percent of youth who participate in 10-day summer program

h Hours stakeholders and lead mentors spend adapting curriculum, policies, goals; percent of stakeholders who respond to feedback surveys

i Strength of relationship and satisfaction reports by mentees, mentors, and parents; engagement assessed by Activity Reflection card input

j Percent of mentors scoring at screening tool thresholds; proportion of high- vs. low-risk mentees involved in CAMP

RESULT OF PROGRAM PARTICIPATION

PROGRAM OUTCOMES

1 Connectedness to school, classmates, culturally different peers, teachers, reading, self-in-the-present, self-in-the-future (self, teacher, and parent reports)

2 Academic self-esteem (extracurricular, peer, teacher, school)

3 Social support from adults at school

4 Social interest

5 Self-reported engagement in violence and misbehavior

6 Academic success as indicated by attendance, class behavior, grades

7 Percent of youth who participate in CAMP in subsequent years as mentees, protégés, mentors, and lead mentors

LONG-TERM IMPACTS

1 Percent assume leadership roles in CAMP

2 Truancy rates

3 Police arrest reports

4 Percent receiving < Ds in middle and high school;

5 Percent graduation

6 Improved teacher-reported school climate and job satisfaction

Program Outcomes and Impact

Average program effect on these outcomes found in prior research on CAMP (d=21) suggest change on outcomes should reflect improvement over one year equal to 20% of a standard deviation on each outcome measure. But CAMP's long-term impact on truancy, drop out, and crime has not been studied previously

FORMATIVE EVALUATION

SUMMATIVE EVALUATION

evaluation yields disappointing results, you have no way of knowing what interfered with key program processes occurring. Conversely, if your program has high fidelity but did not achieve desired changes as a result of the program, you can get a better sense of which program practices were associated with changes (desired or undesired) resulting from the program. We describe high and low fidelity CAMP implementations later in this section. The important point is that you should assess degrees of implementation in a continuous scale (how many attended, what percentage was complete, etc.) rather than dichotomously (did we train mentors, did we use the curriculum, etc.) so that you can conduct these correlations if you choose to.

Factors that affect CAMP implementation

The checklist in Appendix E summarizes many of the implementation points identified above. This list should be gone through prior to initiating your CAMP. That is, once a Program Coordinator thinks all necessary program components are present, then the factors under group I, III, and IV should be reviewed to ascertain the degree to which all are in place. The presence of community level factors (I), program characteristics (III), and organizational readiness and capacity (IV) can each be assessed fairly well before the start of the program—all must be in place prior to starting the CAMP (see Appendix 9b and 9c).

The factors in group II (Provider Characteristics, see Appendix E) also should be reviewed before the program begins to ensure that the necessary training components are planned, as well as midway through the first four months of the program (e.g., in November if the program starts in September) in order to ensure appropriate evaluative feedback is being collected. Several of the key provider (mentor) characteristics are in fact a result of program components (e.g., recruitment, training) and can only be assessed after the program has begun. However, without planning the necessary program components it is quite likely the necessary provider (mentor) characteristics (self-efficacy, necessary skills, hopefulness regarding the interventions effectiveness) will materialize.

A midyear review to assess your program's fidelity

This section can be read as an implementation checklist to assess your program at mid year and see if essential activities and components are in place for your CAMP to operate effectively. As you read through each section, determine whether your program is more like a high or a low-fidelity program, and what can be done to strengthen it. If you have multiple programs (across several schools) or if you want to test the relationship between specific implementation elements and the outcomes you assess for each of the kids later in the outcome evaluation, you can assign a score of 1 to 10 for each category, with 10 being a high-fidelity program implementation and 1 a low-fidelity program implementation score for each mentor, for example. This may help you quantify the implementation evaluation and use it to identify key areas of program needing improvement.

1. Fidelity: the extent to which what you create at your school corresponds to the originally intended program (adherence, compliance, integrity, faithful replication). Does the program you develop look like the one described in this manual?

High-fidelity CAMP: Includes parent involvement, provides prescribed trainings, conducts SuperSaturday events, delivers curricular activities as intended (either as presented in the Curriculum, or as modified or created anew according to the guidelines in the Curriculum), and genuinely involves mentors in a youth-adult partnership that affords opportunities for true leadership, voice, and choice.

Low-fidelity CAMP: Minimal parental involvement (e.g., no SuperSaturdays), chaotic or incomplete utilization of curricular activities or program format (e.g., omits "Touching Base" activity in an attempt to do more academic activities); precludes opportunities for authentic youth participation.

2. Dosage: How much of the original program has been delivered (quantity, intervention strength).

High-dosage CAMP: Mentees participate weekly during the school year (approximately 30 meetings), in quarterly SuperSaturday events (with parents and mentors present), and in summer program. They participate from grades 4–6, are then included during grades 7 and 8 as protégés, and during high school matriculate from new mentor, to advanced mentor, and ideally to Lead Mentor.

Low-dosage CAMP: Mentees participate for only one year, attend none or few of the SuperSaturday and summer events, and attend afterschool meetings inconsistently or their mentors attend inconsistently.

3. Quality refers to how well different program components have been conducted (e.g., are the curricular activities delivered clearly and correctly by mentors?). We note below the presence of elements of Smith's *Youth Program Quality Assessment* (Smith, Peck, Denault, Blazevski & Akiva, 2010) as indicators of high-quality program delivery. Most of these relate to the manner, effectiveness, enthusiasm, concern, and commitment conveyed by mentors and staff.

High-quality delivery of CAMP: Program Coordinators and especially mentors use a warm tone of voice and respectful language; smile, make friendly gestures, and good eye contact; convey the shared traditions of the program and are inclusive in introducing mentees to participate in them; actively encourage mentees to try out the skills being taught; balance the presentation of information with both concepts and concrete examples; effectively encourage mentees to help plan and create activities in as collaborative a manner as possible; provide ample time for reflection on their own work, discussion of others ideas, and presentation of learnings to the group.

Low-quality delivery of CAMP: Program Coordinators and/or mentors associate mostly with each other; demonstrate little interest in adapting the delivery of materials in response to youth suggestions; express flat affect, disinterest, disgust, irritation toward youth; tease youth by making jokes at youth's expense or model similarly disconnecting and deviant behavior by being rude, catty, teasing or harassing each other (directly or in the target person's absence).

4. Participant responsiveness: The degree to which the program stimulates the interest or holds the attention of participants (e.g., are students attentive during program lessons?). Although both mentors and mentees (as well as protégés) are the "consumers" of the program, here we focus on the responsiveness of the mentees, because we assume that where there is high quality delivery of CAMP (described above) there is ample evidence of mentors and protégés' responsiveness (and vice versa—low-quality program delivery indicates mentors' nonresponsiveness to the program).

5. Program differentiation (distinctiveness): The extent to which a program's theory and practices can be distinguished from other programs (program uniqueness). We think the program is quite unique in its use of developmental theory in both design and delivery, the heightened level of SAFE[1] and ongoing training, its inclusion of identified best practices in mentoring (e.g., summer programs, parent involvement), and its explicit efforts to minimize deviancy training. However, these are all matters of design, not delivery. So as long as you are delivering the program as described, you are providing a well-differentiated peer program.

---

1 SAFE stands for sequenced, active, focused, and explicit training, as described by Durlak, Weissberg, & Pachan, 2010.

6. Program reach (participation rates, program scope) refers to the rate of involvement and representativeness of program participants.

Appropriate program reach: Mentees recruited for program participation reflect both academically at-risk and at-promise youth. The proportion of youth at serious risk for misbehavior and delinquent activity is no greater than 1:5, such that in a program of 30 youth, no more than three such youth are involved. Mentors, on average, reflect the youth with the highest scores on the measures of attitudes towards youth, social interest, and empathy.

Inappropriate program reach: Mentees are all at risk academically, behaviorally, socially, and emotionally in such as way as to stigmatize the program and undermine its capacity to influence the youths' participation in conventional and prosocial learning activities. Mentors are not screened for specific attitudes and include a large number of youth who are involved in multiple other extracurricular programs.

7. Adaptation: Changes made in the original program during implementation (program modification, reinvention).

Appropriate program adaptation: Major program changes and modifications are made on the basis of input from multiple stakeholders (teachers, parents, and particularly youth) and are both reviewed and approved by these stakeholders. Major modifications are made deliberately and in accordance with the program logic model (e.g., fostering perspective-taking, connectedness, and social skills [empathy, cooperation, assertiveness, self-restraint]), usually during the summer or during other long breaks when there is sufficient time to consider options for program adaptation and seek input from program stakeholders. Immediate and spontaneous adaptations that are necessary are made in consultation with participating mentors, are theory (logic model) based, and are sufficiently documented in order to make such changes part of the permanent program plan.

Inappropriate program adaptation: Major program changes are made by the program coordinators, without consultation with mentors, school staff or parents. Changes are made based in contextual influences (e.g., who's present, who is demanding something different) primarily with little planning, input from other stakeholders, and limited or unclear connections to the logic model of the program and its targeted goals. Changes, both major and minor are not recorded and incorporated into training and program planning documents, such that their later use is dependent totally on the memories of those involved in making the changes.

Summary of section on implementation

Using the indicators described above, and with the goal of establishing a high-fidelity program before embarking on an outcome evaluation, this first section can help you identify where your program is weak and where it is strong. Sometimes we think the effects of mentoring are simply the result of the match and interaction between mentor and mentee, but really these two players are nested within a larger program, in a school, in a political climate, all of which affect them directly or indirectly. Being sure that all of your program components from staffing and funding, to training and supervision, to attendance and curricular activities are in place is key to delivering a high-quality, high-fidelity, impactful program. Once an adequate degree of fidelity has been achieved and sustained, it is time to turn to your outcomes in the summative evaluation.

Two types of outcome evaluation approaches

If you decide you want to undergo a rigorous evaluation that includes a randomized control group design in which the youth are randomly assigned to the program and to a comparison group, then there are lots of guides available for this. Doing so means you will have a group of youth who are interested in the program but do not receive it (at least not in the year of the evaluation). There are many complex elements to such a design, and for this reason, we suggest this be done by an outside evaluator.

Reasonable alternatives to the fully randomized comparison group design

The alternative designs we suggest are both "quasi-experimental" which means they do not include the element of randomization of participants into comparison and program youth groups. Because it can be very difficult for most programs to conduct participant randomization required for a "gold standard" evaluation, many shift to the other extreme in terms of complexity and rigor. They simply collect pre-post data, which, unfortunately in most cases, is virtually worthless in terms of measuring change. Why? Because it does not provide any evidence of the "counterfactual."

Assessing pre-post change does not give you any evidence of where the participants would have been had they not participated in your program, only where they are at the end of your program. The problem is that program youth may have looked like they do after your program even if they had not participated in your program. There might be changes, but these changes cannot be attributed to your program without some estimate of the counterfactual state (see Grossman, 2005).

We create comparison groups in evaluation to try to estimate what the kids in our program would have looked like had they not been in our program. This is the counterfactual state. The counterfactual is like the "Second life" program in which you pretend to be someone you are not—the counterfactual represents what program youth would look like after the program in an imaginary (counter-to-fact) world in which those youth didn't participate in the program. Ultimately, you want to know, did the program youth benefit from the program? Are they different after the program than they would have been had they not participated in the program?

The "counterfactual state" is actually essential to the program summative or outcome evaluation. Without a good estimate of what your program youth "would" have looked like you just cannot know whether the program made a difference—or, more correctly, whether it is the factor that is truly behind any changes observed among program youth between starting and completing the program. So the question that underlies an effective impact evaluation is "How well have you approximated the counterfactual?"

Warning: Don't watch your mentees get worse

One reason to conduct pre-post comparisons in the program is that there are seasonal differences in the attitudinal outcome measures we use. We know that kids are more connected to school in fall, when they are excited about the new school year, than in spring, when many have cabin fever and can't wait for school to end. So, if you only measure pre-post you will likely see your mentees get worse, not better. As in the original Big Brothers Big Sisters community-based mentoring program, the kids all did more bad stuff after the program; but they did bad stuff less than kids like them who did not participate in mentoring (Grossman & Tierney, 1998). So it is essential that, at least for the school connectedness and academic self-esteem scales, you use a comparison group that provides a good approximation of the counterfactual.

The class cohort comparison group

One way we suggest you estimate the counterfactual state for your program youth is by utilizing already existing groups of youth as your comparison group. This approach is called a *class cohort design*, and it reflects a simple approach. In the class cohort design, you survey intact, whole groups of youth, such as two or three classes of students who are similar in age and general characteristics to your mentees, at the start and conclusion of the program. You can do the same with your mentors (see Karcher, 2009 for example).

These youth do not provide the ideal counterfactual, however, because they are not really the exact kind of youth you target with your program. But, if you follow our guidelines and include a diverse pool of youth who range from being at-risk to at-promise, then the class cohort design may work well. In addition to your outcome measures (e.g., connectedness and self-esteem), you should measure the youth on whatever characteristics differentiate them from your program youth from most kids in the comparison classes.

For example, if, after you follow our guidelines for creating a diverse group of participating CAMP youth, you still find your program youth are, on average, at greater risk for academic underachievement or misbehavior than the one or two classes of students you choose to use in your class cohort design, you can "control" for these. You can measure variables such as grades, school behavior records, or attendance that are associated with (either cause or predict) these risks, then you can have someone with some statistical expertise attempt to "control" for these differences using what's called analysis of covariance.

However, the class cohort comparison is not ideal because even statistical adjustments can't make two groups who are different appear equivalent. Covariance analysis can't really equate the groups; it can only adjust the two groups to be statistically equal on those variables you measured. There will be other unmeasured variables (e.g., family conflict or socioeconomic status) on which it cannot equate the groups. But it can provide a good approximation.

What it does well, however, is give you a sense of how youth in that same school, very much like your program youth, performed between pre and post on the same measures you have included as the focus of your evaluation. It will account for seasonal declines experienced by all youth in the school on the indicators of academic connectedness and self-esteem. I used this approach in my attempt to assess the impact of "being a mentor" on the mentors by conducting between-group difference tests that compared the mentors to two classrooms of their peers (Karcher, 2009).

Matching mentees and comparison youth

Another way you can strengthen the class cohort comparison group design is by conducting a method of matching individual program participants with similar peers in the classroom cohort sample. This matching method is viewed as rigorous and acceptable by many funding organizations, like the Institute for Education Sciences of the U.S. Department of Education, which funds the GEAR UP program. Propensity analysis is the easiest and most rigorous way to select from your comparison group a subsample of youth who match your CAMP participants. It will, however, require the use of an outside evaluator with sufficient statistical knowledge. But the costs in time and money of this approach, and the other benefits of not having a wait list comparison group, likely outweigh the costs of trying to create a comparison group, randomized or not.

Long-term limitations of using a wait-list comparison group

There is one last reason the traditional wait list approach makes the class cohort approach worth considering: the ability to estimate the long-term effects of your program. In the wait list comparison group, the main benefit is that you have a comparison group of kids who are similar to your CAMP mentees in that they want to be in your program—a factor not to be discounted. But, because they want to participate, there may be political consequences of denying them an opportunity to participate. It is difficult to get parents to agree to let you exclude their children the program they desire for their children, so wait list comparison groups are often a way to negotiate this—"if your child is put on the wait list for one year (to serve as the comparison group), your child can then participate in the program." The wait list comparison group allows you to use them as the comparison group (the "counterfactual") one year and provide them the program the next. But this means they cease to be a comparison group in that second year.

Therefore, you cannot estimate the long-term effects of your program when using the wait list design because, ultimately, everyone in your evaluation will get to be a program participant. So you cannot look two, three, four or five years down the road and see if your program and comparison youth differ. At that point, they are all program participants (e.g., Grossman & Tierney 1998; Herrera et al., 2007). So, even in the traditional "gold standard" evaluation designs in which all youth ultimately get the intervention, there are losses incurred with the choice of this rigorous design. You gain a good counterfactual, but you lose the ability to do follow-up studies of program impact. Notice, in fact, that at the time of this publication, there were virtually no long-term follow-up studies of the effects of youth mentoring for this very reason. So this limitation of wait list designs should be a selling point for the class cohort design approach to evaluation.

Final points on the number of program youth needed for the evaluation

Before we wrap up this section on outcome evaluation we need to review the issue and problem of "statistical power," because it has direct and clear implications for how many years you may need to collect data before conducting a reliable test of program outcomes. The main point of this section is to explain why you will need to have a sample of several hundred youth before you can actually conduct outcome analyses.

Statistical power. Statistical power is the degree to which you are likely to find the true effect of the program in your between group comparisons (assuming there is an effect of your program) given the nature of the data and the statistical tests used. Statistical power reflects three things, only one of which is truly under your control. First, there is a chosen level of statistical significance. This is the p-value, which reflects the probability of finding an effect (i.e., a between-group difference on some outcome) of this "size" if in fact there is no real difference (i.e., the program had no effect). It is the chance of finding a difference as large as "X" if in fact there truly is no effect of the program. That is, it is a test of how willing you are to claim a chance difference as true.

Effect size. The second factor in determining the statistical power of your study is the "size" of the impact. This is the difference between the program youth and the control group on some outcome. (It is standardized by dividing this difference by the standard deviation of the youths' scores around the group mean.) This is the standardized difference score, and by convention it ranges from small (.2, reflecting a 1/5 of a standard deviation difference in the group mean scores on a measure between program and control youth) to large (.80, reflecting a 4/5 of a standard deviation difference in means between program and control youth on some outcome). Most mentoring programs yield a "small" effect (See DuBois, Holloway, Valentine, & Cooper, 2002; DuBois, Portillo, Rhodes, Silverthorne, & Valentine, 2011). By the way, we mean small in terms of social science measurements, not necessarily small in terms of its ultimate impact on youth's lives. Of course, it's arguable that you could have some control over the size of the program effect by running a better program, which is true. But when planning a study or an evaluation, it is prudent to assume your program will have a similar size impact to most other well-run mentoring programs, "small."

Sample size. The third factor is sample size. Aside from how well you run your program, this is the only factor over which you have control. In short, more is better, and many more than you might assume are necessary to have an adequately powered test. Adequately powered, from a research perspective, is a statistical test wherein you run the risk of not finding an effect (that really exists) only 1 in 5 times you ran the study. If you ran the study 100 or 1000 times, would you find the effect 80 percent of the time?

The sample size required to capture a small effect (1/5th of a standard deviation difference) between two groups would be around 300 youth in the program and 300 youth in the comparison (counterfactual) groups. (This assumes you include a few covariate variables in the analyses like prior attendance and GPA.) If you run a program that includes 60 youth a year (e.g., 15 mentor-mentee pairs meeting once a week, Monday through Thursday, which is a lot), it could take you five years to achieve the sample size you need in order to reliably test the effects of your program. So, you may not agree you can wait that long, but you should give consideration to whether or not you can collect data for two or three years before running the analyses to boost your statistical power.

Conclusion

This chapter has overviewed the elements of evaluation, but more importantly it has listed the key elements of the formative evaluation of the program's fidelity of implementation. This chapter and the associated appendices also attempt to provide step-by-step instructions, checklists, and specific procedures for undertaking a full evaluation. In the appendix we list the surveys and checklists to be used, time lines for when to implement each, and methods for scoring and interpreting them.

In this chapter we have tried to explain that measuring outcomes for youth is not all of what has to happen in the evaluation. The implementation and process evaluations (part of the formative evaluation) are essential to a healthy program. We've tried to explain the importance of measuring program fidelity, which is done in the formative evaluation, and of linking the presence of specific program activities to intermediate process (or proximal) outcomes that measure whether CAMP activities are having their intended effects.

Not until you have achieved your goals and thereby are sure you are evaluating the "program of your dreams" (in its desired form) should you shift to the outcome evaluation. This may take multiple years to achieve, but don't allow yourself to feel that you are not "evaluating" your program because you have not undergone the outcome evaluation. The formative evaluation is arguably a far more important and essential evaluation than is the outcome evaluation. The formative evaluation helps you inch toward a stronger program, and the evidence collected through the formative evaluation is also arguably much more reliable evidence of program quality than is the evidence yielded from an outcome evaluation. So take the formative evaluation seriously, and your program will profit greatly.

Outcomes are important, however. But we shared several reasons why the traditional experimental, control group evaluation is hard to do for most CAMP coordinators and other approaches may be more viable. We suggested that the class cohort design can provide outcome data that are just as valuable as those gathered using a traditional, experimental design; for some programs they may provide much less costly evaluations. Conducting these evaluations, both the formative evaluation which can take several years and the subsequent summative evaluation of program outcomes which requires multiple years of data as well, is a long-term commitment. Simply, it cannot be done all in one year. But by viewing evaluation as a part of program design and itself a necessary program activity (in a high fidelity, high quality program), it should become part of what happens all across the year every year. When organized and distributed across the year, assessments conducted on a regular basis can be done easily and provide sufficient information to not only assess whether the program is having an impact, but how it is reaching its effects, and how the program can be strengthened.

APPENDICES

THE DISTANCE MODEL: AN ALTERNATIVE WAY TO STRUCTURE CAMP

In this model, there are nine daylong Saturday meetings between mentors and mentees between fall and spring. The Saturday meetings provide both academic enrichment classes, typically in the morning, and social connectedness activities in the afternoons. The primary goal of the monthly Saturday meetings is to develop the mentoring relationships, to help children become accustomed to the structure and goals of the program, and to provide an ongoing social experience where interpersonal connectedness and academic studies are integrated.

This model may be ideal when schools want to provide outreach into communities their students rarely have access to. Such was the case for the Stephen's Kids program in Austin (Karcher, Davis, & Powell, 2002), where students in a boarding school outside of town worked with students from downtown public schools. The most challenging issue for these programs is transportation. Even if one or the other school provides a bus to get the students to and from each school, parents may have to bring their children to designated place in order to reduce the total travel time the bus has to incur to pick up the children and deliver them to the program, and again to get the youth home. It is this travel time and transportation issue that makes it easiest for schools that are far away from each other to meet just one Saturday a month during the academic year.

One structure for meetings: Climbing up the developmental ladder

Whether taking place after school or on Saturdays, all CAMP meetings follow the same basic form. The meetings begin with a group icebreaker, then the group splits into mentor-mentee pairs to share experiences since the last meeting, and to then to work on a Listen and Learn activity. This activity is followed by a snack, after which a Core Activity takes place where the mentoring dyad typically join the larger group of kids either to create something together or to engage in some activity that helps foster a positive peer culture.

We call this sequence, "Walking the match up the developmental ladder" every time they meet. This is much like Ivey's "developmental counseling" (1986) but is based more explicitly on Selman and Schultz's (1990) developmental model and intervention approach. The idea here is that we walk youth through activities that elicit each of the developmental stages that occur naturally between childhood and adolescence. This helps to provide a foundation for some of the more complex activities that occur later in the meeting time.

Finally, in the last few minutes of the meeting a group game or activity (e.g., doing artwork or playing basketball) takes place. We find that allowing some fairly unstructured time toward the end of the day makes it easier for parents who either arrive early or later than the formal ending of the program. This flexible play time can be interrupted or extended and morphed into different groups to accommodate parent's arrival times.

During the bulk of the meeting, mentees meet individually with their mentors, working on CAMP curriculum. This curriculum is broken into themes which promote connectedness to a particular "world," such as family, school, peers, friends, self or reading. While the curriculum is used to structure the pair, the relationship between them is always what is most important. In fact, the curriculum is designed to be flexible and often is adapted considerably by the mentors themselves as a way to gain their "buy-in" to the use of such activities. These activities and the guidelines used for selecting and adapting them are presented later in this manual and more fully in the accompanying "CAMP Curriculum." To fully understand the content and goals of the curriculum requires a fuller understanding of the specific developmental theories described in Chapter 2 and the theories and methods supporting the connectedness promotion activities, which are covered in a later chapter as well.

Shape of the year

Over the course of the school year, a given program will recruit mentors and mentees, conduct the pretest evaluation, conduct mentor training, facilitate a self-matching process between mentors and mentees (the Meet-and-Greet), meet regularly to work through the connectedness curricula, facilitate the "termination ritual" to guide matches to a mutually satisfactory close, assess mentee development using a posttest evaluation, and conduct the summer program. A summary of these procedures is presented in the table below, and is reviewed in much greater detail in this manual.

Time Period	Task	CAMP Resource
Early September	Locate mentors and mentees	Program Manual
Late September	Mentor training (and mentor pretest on SIS and Hemingway measures)	Training Guide
Early October	Mentee orientation and initial assessment	Program Manual
Mid-October	Mee-and-Greet (matching)	Program Manual
October–April	Regular mentor meetings	Curriculum
Late spring	Recruit mentors for fall, recruit mentees for summer	Program Manual
Late April	End-of-year assessment	
	Practice goodbyes and then do actual Match Termination ritual	Program Manual
June	Summer program	Curriculum

Recruiting of mentees and mentors takes place at the end of the spring, and, when necessary, again at the beginning of the school year. Sometimes the recruiting takes place in the fall, but considerable "mentoring" time can be lost when the start of the fall is when the Program Coordinator initiates the extended process of getting teacher nominations (especially from teachers who don't yet know their students), introducing the program to the youth and their parents, securing consent forms (along with schedules for transportation and matching), and then matching. CAMP's *Program Manual* provides a number of resources to help the program coordinator carry out this task, which may help speed up the process initially. The manual includes tips on recruiting strategies, sample follow-up letters to mentors, parents, teachers, and other stakeholders, and materials explaining the benefits of the program to all potential participants. However, we find that if recruitment can take place in the late spring, the summer provides a more flexible time period for doing some of the essential preparatory work.

Mentees are best recruited in the spring when teachers are most aware of their students' needs and achievement. Both youth at low risk and youth at high risk for peer problems or academic disengagement (but not academic deficits, for whom tutoring may be a better route) should be recruited in order to avoid stigmatizing the program and fostering deviancy training (Dishion, McCord, & Poulin, 1999). By recruiting in the spring you can introduce some youth to the program in the summer and thereby start to integrate the new youth into a collective culture of positive peer relationships by integrating some new youth into the existing group of mentees. Although mentors and mentees won't be matched formally until early fall, they can interact with each other during the summer meetings, become acquainted and comfortable with the program, and then matched in the fall. This also helps avoid failed matches that can occur when mentor or mentees' first experiences of the program are in the fall right as matches are made. Students who opt out in the summer, before they have been matched, don't suffer any harm from failed matches. This can make the introduction of youth, both mentors and mentees, a bit more chaotic and require good records of which students are involved when; but the advantages of entering youth in stages increases the likelihood that the culture that is established in the program one year is not disrupted the next year when half of the students are totally new to the program.

The initial assessment

An assessment of connectedness and self-esteem (for mentees, and social interest and attitudes towards youth for mentors) is conducted early in the year for both mentors and mentees. The mentoring program aims to increase the mentees' connectedness to the people and places in their lives, and in order to demonstrate change, a pre- and postassessment is needed. When the program is undergoing an evaluation that includes a comparison group of youth who were randomly selected to not participate (as well as who are allowed to participate), this pretest surveying needs to be done before the youth are aware of their program status. This is explained more in the chapter on evaluation, and it complicates the process of allowing some youth to start in summer and some to start in fall, but when the impact evaluation is conducted the results are well worth the added complexity of doing the recruitments somewhat differently.

Assessments are not only used for impact evaluations, but also for process evaluations as well as for mentor self-assessments, staff assessments of youth needs, and sometimes mentors' edification about the uniqueness of their mentees. The mentors take the Social Interest Survey to help them understand their own potential strengths and weaknesses as mentors. Mentees and mentors take the Hemingway Measure of Connectedness to get a baseline for showing progress during the course of the mentoring program. The *Hemingway Measure of Connectedness* is a self-report survey of 75 items used to assess the level of connectedness a youth reports across a variety of "worlds," including family, school, friends, peers, and self (these are the same worlds of connectedness targeted by the CAMP curriculum). This measure, described in Karcher, Holcomb, and Zambano (2008) is easy to use and interpret. There is a shorter version (52 items, with four fewer scales) and a childhood version for grades 3–6.

Apart from its use in estimating youths' progress during the program on each connectedness domain, though, this initial assessment also helps the program coordinator determine which worlds the mentees are most disconnected from when entering the program. With this information, the coordinator can choose curriculum that will address areas where mentees need the most help.

Mentor training

A theory-based mentor training is conducted using the *CAMP Training Guide*. The *Training Guide* leads the person in charge of mentor training with examples, activities, and group discussion. This training usually takes a full day, and helps mentors understand both their responsibilities and the structure of the program. Studies have shown that high school mentors who understand that their role is to provide empathy, praise, and attention within a clear, consistent structure will be most effective. The program is unique in the rigorous training and strong structure it provides for mentors.

When the training is to be provided is partly determined by when the mentor starts. If a mentor who was recruited in the spring wants to participate in the summer event, then they go through the training before the summer program. If she does not want to start to mentor until the fall, then she gets the training in the fall. While there is some loss of group cohesiveness by having multiple training times, there are benefits to training small groups of mentors at a time, and of having the advanced and lead mentors participate in the training repeatedly. The small groups likely facilitate better learning and more direct interaction with program staff. Because the training can be done using a subset of a larger group of training activities, mentors can attend multiple trainings and each time participate in different activities. The repeated experience of advanced and Lead Mentors allow them to master the content and take an ownership in the training by being able to serve as cotrainers.

The mentor-mentee matching process

The matching process used in CAMP also is unique. The Meet-and-Greet is a way to encourage a good fit between mentor and mentee by capitalizing on the interpersonal qualities that draw people together (as happens in natural mentoring). At the first mentoring meeting, the whole group engages in icebreakers and activities that help the program participants get to know each other. At the end of the meeting, each participant writes down a list of three people he or she remembers and enjoyed spending time with. With this process, I have found that the vast majority of mentees end up being paired with either the first or second person they recalled and noted on their lists. This process leverages natural interactions to create self-selected matches, which we believe have a better chance of surviving in the long run.

Mentor and mentee meetings

Mentors and mentees meet throughout the school year, although the frequency and length of these meetings depends on the type of program the CAMP coordinator selects. Of the two models described above, the proximity (or close-by campus model) model that is described in the larger manual is the most common. It's called the proximity or "close-by" model because the mentors and mentees attend nearby schools in the same district. In this case, it is possible for mentoring meetings to occur weekly after school for about one and a half to two hours. In addition to these during or afterschool meetings, three or four half-day long meetings take place on Saturdays every other month and parents are encouraged to attend. When implementing the distance model, afterschool meetings are impractical due to the distance between the schools. In this case, program participants have daylong meetings once a month on Saturday. Both the afterschool (close by model) and the Saturday-only (distance model) meetings follow the same basic structure of "walking up the developmental ladder" discussed above in "Shape of a Meeting."

The match termination ritual

The program holds a "cup half empty" view of the limited number of matches that continue from one year to the next. We emphasize a "do no harm" approach that seeks to minimize the negative effects of poorly ended matches on those at greater risk to be harmed by such failed matches. The Herrera, Knuh, Cooney, Grossman, and McMaken (2008) study can be read as an indication that if you insist on only multiple-year matches as being a success—if that is your gold standard—then you are dooming half of your kids to failure and a loss that is often out of their control. Usually, it is the half who need the help the most who are disproportionately more likely to experience the failed match (Grossman & Rhodes, 2002). Knowing that only half of the mentees will be rematched in the fall with their same mentor leads us to emphasize instead the developmentally critical life lesson of learning how to say goodbye. We want to make sure every match has multiple chances to reflect on and celebrate their successes at the end of the year. This makes continuing those matches—at least, as an explicit goal—dubious and confusing to the youth. Rather, we want to close all of the matches successfully in the spring, and restart any desiring to continue in the fall, when the appropriate time comes to do that: In the fall.

For these reasons we formalize the termination ritual as one of the essential end of year activities, and we utilize a practice termination ritual called a "relationship reflection" a few weeks prior. This helps to ensure that the mentor and mentee have sufficient time and structured opportunity to articulate and then psychologically integrate their respective views on the course of their relationship during the year. Even when there may have been difficult times that get discussed, however the mentor frames those struggles (and they are coached ahead of time in how to do this), rarely would the mentor say anything worse than the some of negative thoughts the youth would generate—driven by self-criticism, self-doubt—for understanding how those events were related to the inevitable ending of their relationship.

The Match Termination Ritual is used to help mentoring matches come to a positive conclusion. Although some matches may last for several years, at some point most mentors will graduate, begin to work, or go to college, or they or their mentees will transfer to another school. In some cases, matches may have to end for more interpersonal reasons, such as difficulty communicating or a lack of trust between the mentor and mentee. Whatever the reason, when a match ends it is important for both the mentor and the mentee to reflect on the positive and negative aspects of relationship. We use a termination ritual and a relationship reflection activity in the spring to accomplish this because we feel the benefits of helping youth experience a successful goodbye—especially youth who have so often in the past had little control over the losses of important people in their lives—is a far superior (and a more realistic) goal than hoping that all matches will continue ad infinitum when we know from research that most won't.

The end-of-year assessment

An end-of-year assessment is conducted, typically through a survey (though at times interviews may be more revealing) to assess both mentee and mentors' relationship quality, mentors' perceptions of program support, and mentor and mentees' outcomes on connectedness and self-esteem (for mentees, social interest for mentors). These data are used to estimate changes in levels of connectedness and self-esteem over the course of the program, and also to get feedback on the program as a whole. The changes in these outcomes resulting from this final assessment can be used to gauge the relationship between specific practices or mentor traits and program success. These data can be used to fine-tune the program for the following school year. With these data in hand, the CAMP coordinator can report any progress for individual mentees and the program as a whole using empirical data. These data can be used to show parents of current and prospective participants what the program can achieve and to secure new sources of funding for the program continuation (when results are positive!) or program retooling (when the results are negative).

There are a number of reasons that typically have precluded many programs from conducting their own evaluations. Often, programs don't know what measures to use, or use measures somewhat unrelated to the areas the program impacts, or the staff don't know how to administer or score the measures used. Equally, if not more often, program staff members don't know what to do with the data once they have it, or how to collect it in a fashion that is minimally intrusive and maximally valid for the sort of "change" interpretations or statements that the program wants to make. To address these concerns, see the evaluation chapter which answers each of these questions. We feel CAMP Coordinators can generate high-quality program evaluations and process evaluations of the relationship between different program components and specific programmatic outcomes. For those who would prefer to hand their data over to local evaluators or university faculty for analysis, we have included in the appendix the necessary scoring information and scoring syntax that can be used in the Statistical Package for the Social Sciences (SPSS) program commonly used by university researchers.

The CAMP summer program

Summer CAMP allows those mentors and mentees who continue from the fall to strengthen and develop their relationships in an intensive, two-week period. For new youth, or youth whose partners (mentor or mentee) are unable to participate in the summer CAMP, this program component serves as a booster session to help maintain program impact (see Herrera et al., 2007), interest by mentors and mentees, and the collective, positive peer culture.

Participants meet 6 to 10 days for up to seven hours a day. Although this period is much more academically intensive than the rest of the school year, the daily meetings follow the same basic shape as the regular meetings during the school year. All participants are strongly encouraged to continue meeting for the summer program, which is an excellent opportunity for mentors and mentees to really get to know each other through joint involvement in field trips, sports and crafts activities, and daily interactions in the academic context.

Very often some program participants may not be able to meet during the summer for various reasons. The program has guidelines for how to find alternative matches or other workarounds for these situations. But in general, small groups and part-time dyads are set up in the summer. In the summer CAMP, there will be new mentors who have just been trained, and sometimes there will be new mentees. For the most part, the new mentors and mentees begin in the fall and are matched using the Meet-and-Greet procedure at that time. However, sometimes matches that are formed naturally, albeit temporarily, during the summer become formal matches in the fall (when each person names the other as their most memorable person). But in the summer, matches are downplayed to some extent by involving more individual and group assignments so that those youth whose mentors or mentees aren't present don't feel bad or left out.

It is reasonable to ask why there is this flexibility or ambiguity about the summer program and whether or not there will be new mentors and mentees introduced at this time. It is because in practice, we have found that the number of youth who cannot participate in the summer precludes fully retaining all of the dyad matches from the prior school year, and rather than try to force this, it can be more reasonable to include whomever can attend and focus on building community over intensifying the formal mentoring relationships.

A second reason the summer is a bit less dyad-focused is because the termination ritual which is practiced and implemented in the spring makes it odd if not awkward to try to keep matches together when they have all just closed down for the summer. In contrast, the Big Brothers Big Sisters of America High School Bigs program focuses on longer and stronger matches as their goal. This is partly due to their reading of the Herrera et al. (2007, 2008) impact studies, which revealed that matches that continued into the second year both retained their benefits and had bigger benefits than those matches that did not. The problem with this interpretation, however, is that the mentees whose matches continued into the second year were easier kids to mentor. The more difficult-to-mentor youth were more likely to not be rematched in the second year. For this reason, it is not a true test of the effects of longer matches as much as these findings are a test of the effects of easier matches. We know less at-risk youth benefit more from mentoring and that they retain their mentors more often both in the community (Grossman & Rhodes, 2002) and in the schools (Herrera's studies). Their emphasis on making all matches longer and stronger is laudable, but may reflect a "cup half-full" approach which neglects the impact of failed matches on the other half of the mentees in who have spilled out of that cup.

Appendix B. Sample CAMP Policies and Procedure Forms

Memorandum of Understanding

This Memorandum of Understanding (MOU) made this _____ day of _____, _____ as managed by the Cross-Age Mentoring Program (CAMP) establishes that CAMP will agree to the following terms and conditions as partners:

CAMP will:

- Identify, solicit, and recruit volunteer mentor applicants

- Manage programmatic activities including but not limited to development of policies and procedures, fund development, and match management

- Oversee all operational activities including screening, training, matching, support and supervision, recognition, and closure procedures

- Coordinate mentor and mentee matching to meet the goal of 25 new matches per year

- Provide annual evaluation summaries of the project to all partners

- Serve as the primary agency for group recreational activities and games

- Provide training to mentors and program staff

School district will:

- Provide an adequate project site, office space, and necessary facility amenities

- Identify appropriate CAMP students for referral as mentors and mentees

- Advise on the academic needs of participating youth

- Assist in providing program evaluation data on participating students including grades, attendance records, discipline records, and counselor and teacher reports

- Provide a contact person or liaison

- Cooperate to the fullest extent possible with CAMP Coordinator

CAMP will hold all information confidential regarding participants and release such information only with signed parental consent or in cooperation with law enforcement investigations in compliance with local and state laws and statutes. In witness whereof, the parties hereto have caused this MOU to be executed as of the day and year listed below.

Cross-Age Mentoring Program:

Name _____ Title _____ Date _____

School District:

Name _____ Title _____ Date _____

Name _____ Title _____ Date _____

Program Coordinator Job Description

The Program Coordinator oversees the development and implementation of the CAMP mentoring program, which matches volunteer teen mentors with youth in a one-to-one relationship. The Program Coordinator ensures program quality and performance related to recruiting, screening, matching, monitoring, and closing the relationship with the mentor and child, and communicates with the mentor, parent/guardian, and child throughout the relationship. The Program Coordinator is responsible for overseeing all aspects of the mentoring program, and will carry out the responsibilities of the position as defined below:

Duties:

- Create and oversee implementation of an ongoing mentor recruitment plan, including development of annual recruitment and quarterly activity plans, development and distribution of program marketing materials, presentations to targeted organizations, and presence at key community events, etc.

- Perform and oversee participant screening, training, matching, support and supervision, recognition, and closure activities

- Develop and manage relationships with schools, training centers, and community-based organizations

- Create and build a strong working relationship with a mentoring program advisory board

- Manage the planning and implementation of mentor/mentee meetings, both after school, on SuperSaturdays and during summer activities (e.g., bowling trips, pizza parties, end-of-year events)

- Plan and implement recognition activities for program participants

- Maintain and update the program's policy and procedure manual as needed

- Oversee program evaluation activities

- Supervise mentoring program Lead Mentors, mentors, and protégés

- Attend conferences to increase knowledge of mentoring program and best practices

- Complete other duties and activities as needed

Qualifications:

- Bachelor's degree preferred with emphasis on social work, psychology, volunteer management, and/or education
- Two or more years' experience in mentoring and youth development, teaching experiences or working within community organizations and/or schools preferred
- Expert knowledge of mentoring program policies and procedures
- Extremely strong organizational, writing, verbal, and interpersonal skills
- Creativity and flexibility in assuming significant responsibility
- Experience working in ethnically and socioeconomically diverse urban communities preferred
- Spanish speaking/writing preferred

Compensation:

Applications: A letter of application and résumé should be submitted to:

Mentor Job Description

Cross-Age Mentoring Program (CAMP) helps to empower youth in our community to make positive life choices that enable them to maximize their potential. The mentoring program uses old peer mentors to commit to supporting, guiding, and being a friend to a young person for a period of at least one year. By becoming part of the social network of community members who care about the youth, the mentor can help youth develop and reach positive academic, career, and personal goals.

Mentor role

- Take the lead in supporting a young person through an ongoing, one-to-one relationship
- Serve as a positive role model and friend
- Build the relationship by planning and participating in activities together
- Strive for mutual respect
- Build self-esteem and motivation
- Help set goals and work toward accomplishing them
- Provide guidance, social support and limited academic assistance

Time commitment

- Make a one-year commitment
- Spend a minimum of eight hours per month one-to-one with a mentee
- Communicate with the mentee weekly
- Attend an initial two-hour training session and additional two-hour training sessions twice during each year of participation in the program
- Attend the weekly meetings and SuperSaturday events throughout the year
- Inform the Program Coordinator if unable to make a match meeting
- Attend all orientation and trainings (including ongoing training)
- Follow all program guidelines on mentor behavior (staying on task, being respectful, modeling positive behaviors, focusing on the mentee, etc..)
- Complete all evaluation surveys and other program paperwork
- Report on match activities and provide other feedback as required

Participation requirements

- Be at least a freshman in high school
- Be interested in working with young people
- Be willing to adhere to all program policies and procedures
- Be willing to complete the application and screening process
- Be dependable and consistent in meeting the time commitments
- Attend mentor training sessions as prescribed
- Be willing to communicate regularly with program staff, submit activity information, and take constructive feedback regarding mentoring activities
- Have a clean criminal history
- Have no history of use of illicit drugs, alcohol, or controlled substances
- Not currently in treatment for a mental disorder or substance use or hospitalized for such in the past three years
- Not in the senior year of high school or planning not be enrolled in the school for the full year

Desirable qualities

- Interpersonal competence, integrity, and stability

- Willing listener
- Encouraging and supportive
- Patient, flexible, and other-centered
- Tolerant and respectful of individual differences
- Able to commit to programs, people, and projects even when there are other demands in their lives
- Skilled in friendship development and maintenance
- Interested in sharing information and empowering others to develop skills and talents
- Good communication, listening, and problem-solving skills
- Interested in working with youth
- Aspires to a career in the helping professions
- Able to have fun with others in both structured and unstructured settings

Benefits

- Personal fulfillment through contribution to the community and individuals
- Satisfaction in helping someone mature, progress, and achieve goals
- Training sessions and group activities
- Participation in a mentor support group
- Personal ongoing support and supervision to help the match succeed
- Mentee/mentor group activities, complementary tickets to community events, and participant-recognition events
- Skills in perspective taking
- A greater sense of connectedness

Application and screening process

- Written application
- Criminal history check: state, child abuse and neglect registry, sexual offender registry
- Personal interview
- Provide three personal references
- Attend two-hour mentor training
- Must complete *Hemingway Measure of Adolescent Connectedness*
- Must complete *Social Interest Scale* and *Mentor Attitudes Towards Youth* measurements

Lead Mentor Job Description

Cross-Age Mentoring Program (CAMP) helps to empower youth in our community to make positive life choices that enable them to maximize their potential. The mentoring program uses experienced peer mentors to commit to supporting, guiding, and training other mentors with less experience. Lead mentors lead, develop activities, provide constructive criticism, and help out.

Lead Mentor role

- Report any match problems or program feedback to the Program Coordinator. Lead Mentors are a critical communicator between program participants and the adults in charge of the program.
- Serve as a "temporary" mentor if mentors miss a weekly meeting or SuperSaturday. Lead Mentors can step in and make sure that no mentee is without a partner for that day.
- Assist with mentor recruitment and the development of program materials, such as posters or handouts.
- Help to deliver the mentor training. Delivering actual training content builds their skills, and sharing their insights into what it's like to be a mentor in the program can be invaluable to a new batch of mentors.
- Inform mentors about upcoming events and ensuring attendance at the afterschool and SuperSaturday events.
- Help disseminate and collect program paperwork, such as permission slips for a group outing or surveys.
- Work with the Program Coordinator to improve the curriculum and identify needed adjustments to existing activities. Lead Mentors can also help develop new activities that fit with CAMP goals and philosophies.
- Follow all program guidelines on mentor behavior (staying on task, being respectful, modeling positive behaviors, focusing on the mentee, etc.)
- Complete all evaluation surveys and other program paperwork.
- Report on match activities and provide other feedback as required.

Time commitment

- Make a one-year commitment
- Attend an initial summer training session and additional monthly supervision sessions
- Attend the weekly meetings and SuperSaturday events throughout the year
- Inform the Program Coordinator if unable to make a match meeting
- Attend all orientations and trainings (including ongoing training of mentors)

Participation requirements

- Be at least a sophomore in high school
- Be interested in working with young people
- Be willing to adhere to all program policies and procedures
- Be willing to complete the application and screening process
- Be dependable and consistent in meeting the time commitments
- Be willing to communicate regularly with program staff, submit activity information, and take constructive feedback regarding mentoring activities
- Have a clean criminal history
- Refrain from use of illicit drugs, alcohol or other controlled substances

Desirable qualities

- Demonstrate interpersonal competence, integrity, and stability
- Be a willing listener, encouraging and supportive
- Be supportive, patient, flexible, and other centered
- Be tolerant and respectful of individual differences
- Commit to prioritizing the program, even when there are other demands in their lives
- Be skilled in friendship development and maintenance
- Be interested in sharing information and empowering others to develop skills and talents
- Possess good communication, listening, and problem-solving skills
- Be interested in working with youth
- Aspire to career in the helping professions
- Be able to have fun with others in both structured and unstructured settings
- Be willing to assume leadership roles

Benefits

- Personal fulfillment through contribution to the community and individuals
- Satisfaction in helping someone mature, progress, and achieve goals
- Training sessions and group activities
- Participation in a mentor support group
- Personal ongoing support, supervision to help the match succeed
- Mentee/mentor group activities, complimentary tickets to community events, participant recognition events
- Skills in perspective taking and greater sense of connectedness
- Demonstrated recognition as a leader

Application and screening process

- Written application
- Criminal history check: state, child abuse and neglect registry, sexual offender registry
- Personal interview
- Three personal references
- Completed *Hemingway Measure of Adolescent Connectedness*
- Completed *Social Interest Scale* and *Mentor Attitudes Towards Youth* measurements

Mentor Application

(please print)

Date _____

Name of applicant _____ Birth date _____ SS# _____

Address _____

City _____ State _____ ZIP _____

Home phone _____ E-mail _____

Employer _____ Occupation _____

Address _____

City _____ State _____ ZIP _____

Business: Phone _____ Fax _____ E-mail _____

Preferred mentoring day (Mon–Fri): Choice #1 _____ Choice #2 _____

Do you prefer to be matched with: (circle)   boy   girl   no preference

I would like to work with a child in grade: (circle) Elementary: K 1 2 3 4 5 Middle School: 6 7 8

What you bring: What's unique about you?

Write a brief statement on why you wish to be a mentor in the program:

Describe special interests/hobbies, which may be helpful in matching you with a mentee (e.g., cooking, crafts, career interests, chess, stamp collecting, sports such as baseball or football, computers, art, needlepoint, speak another language, music, painting):

Mentor's Possible Skill Areas: Here, let the mentor list some of her/his skill areas.

Sports:
Art or creative skill:
Language:
Experiences (work, college, new contexts):

Activities I'd Like To Do or Learn and Practice When We Meet (circle)

photography	art	drawing	painting	libraries	reading
crafts	sewing	science	spirituality	puzzles	math
history	writing stories	writing	poetry	other:	
games:	chess	checkers	cards	board games	computer job search

Things I'd Like To Discuss or Learn About (circle)

football	singing	movies	yoga	reading	cars	pets
basketball	tennis	animals	running	swimming	baseball	horses
museums/art	wrestling	soccer	rugby	cards	ballet	poetry
racquetball	shopping	music	art	crafts	sewing	writing
writing stories	libraries	hiking	dancing	cooking	camping	history
gymnastics	soccer	computer	plays/acting	spirituality	TV	softball
amusement parks	bowling	concerts	fishing	science	nature	math
photography	other:					

In school, my FAVORITE subjects are (Circle at least one even if school isn't your favorite thing):

Social Studies   Science   PE   Art   Math   English   Music
Language Arts   other:

In school, my WORST subjects are (Circle at least one—even if you rock in all your classes):

Social Studies   Science   PE   Art   Math   English   Music
Language Arts   Other:

Next, choose the description from each pair that best reflects what best explains who you would rather be. For each pair of personal characteristics or traits, circle the trait which you value more highly. In making each choice, ask yourself which of the traits in that pair you would rather possess as one of your own characteristics. For example, the first pair is "imaginative—rational." If you had to make a choice, which would you rather be?

"I would rather be …"

imaginative	or	rational		neat	or	logical
helpful	or	quick-witted		forgiving	or	gentle
neat	or	sympathetic		efficient	or	respectful
level-headed	or	efficient		practical	or	self-confident
intelligent	or	considerate		capable	or	independent
self-reliant	or	ambitious		alert	or	cooperative
respectful	or	original		imaginative	or	helpful
creative	or	sensible		realistic	or	moral
generous	or	individualistic		considerate	or	wise
responsible	or	original		sympathetic	or	individualistic
capable	or	tolerant		ambitious	or	patient
trustworthy	or	wise		reasonable	or	quick-witted

How many kids in your community …

	None	Very Few	Some	Many	All or almost all
Work hard at school					
Respect adults					
Are troublemakers					
Are fun to be around					
Expect things to be handed to them					
Try to do their best					
Are interested in learning					

Mentor Personal/Employment History and Release Statement

State the addresses where you have lived for the last five years (begin with the most recent, not counting your current address):

Dates _____ Address _____

City _____ State _____ ZIP _____

Dates _____ Address _____

City _____ State _____ ZIP _____

Please provide two personal references (other than family members):

1. Name _____ Phone _____ Relationship _____

Address _____ City _____ State _____ ZIP _____

2. Name _____ Phone _____ Relationship _____

Address _____ City _____ State _____ ZIP _____

Employment History

List the last two places of employment or persons you worked for:

1. Company/Person _____ Address _____

City _____ State _____ ZIP _____

Dates of employment _____ to _____ Can we contact them to ask about you? Yes or No?

2. Company/Person _____ Address _____

City _____ State _____ ZIP _____

Dates of employment _____ to _____ Can we contact them to ask about you? Yes or No?

Application Questions

Please answer all of the following questions as completely as possible. If more space is needed, use an extra sheet of paper or write on the back of this page.

1. Why do you want to become a mentor?

2. Do you have any previous experience volunteering or working with youth? If so, please specify.

3. What qualities, skills, or other attributes do you have that would benefit a youth? Please explain.

4. Can you commit to participate in the Cross-Age Mentoring Program for a minimum of one year from the time you are matched with a youth?

5. Are you available to meet with a child eight hours per month and have contact at least once per week? Please explain any particular scheduling issues.

6. Describe your general health. Are you currently under a physician's care or taking any medications? If so, please explain.

7. How would you describe yourself as a person?

8. How would your friends, family, and fellow students describe you?

9. Have you ever been arrested or convicted of a crime? If so, what were the circumstances?

10. Have you ever been in trouble for or received treatment for alcohol or substance abuse? If yes, please explain.

11. Have you ever been treated or hospitalized for a mental disorder? If yes, please explain.

12. Have you ever been investigated or convicted of child abuse or neglect? If yes, please explain.

13. Have you ever been investigated or convicted of sexually abusing or molesting a youth 18 or younger? If yes, please explain.

14. Are you willing to communicate regularly and openly with program staff, provide monthly information regarding your mentoring activities, and receive feedback regarding any difficulties during your participation in the mentoring program?

15. Are you willing to attend an initial mentor training session and two in service training sessions per year after being matched?

Please read this carefully before signing:

Cross-Age Mentoring Program appreciates your interest in becoming a mentor.

Please initial each of the following:

_____ I agree to follow all mentoring program guidelines and understand that any violation will result in suspension and/or termination of the mentoring relationship.

_____ I understand that Cross–age Mentoring Program is not obligated to provide a reason for its decision in accepting or rejecting me as a mentor.

_____ (optional) I agree to allow Cross-Age Mentoring Program to use any photographic image of me taken while participating in the mentoring program. These images may be used in promotions or other related marketing materials.

I understand I must return all of the following completed items along with this application, and that any incomplete information will result in the delay of my application being processed:

By signing below, I attest to the truthfulness of all information listed on this application and agree to all the above terms and conditions.

Signature _____ Date _____

Please return or mail this application and the items listed above to:

Lead Mentor Application (Supplement to Mentor Application)

(please print)

Date _____

Name of applicant _____ Birth date _____ SS# _____

Address _____

City _____ State _____ ZIP _____

Home phone _____ Home e-mail _____

Employer _____ Occupation _____

Address _____

City _____ State _____ ZIP _____

Business: Phone _____ Fax _____ E-mail _____

Preferred mentoring day (Mon–Fri): Choice #1 _____ Choice #2 _____

Best time of day to mentor (circle all that apply):   morning   afternoon   evening

Why do you wish to be a lead mentor in the program?

Describe special experiences or leadership skills that would make you a good lead mentor.

By signing below, I attest to the truthfulness of all information listed on this application and agree to all the above terms and conditions.

Signature _____ Date _____

Please return or mail this application and the items listed above to:

Mentee Application

(To Be Completed by the Parent/Guardian)

Youth's name _____ Date _____

Parent/guardian name _____

Relationship to youth: __ Mother __ Father __ Other, specify _____

Address _____

City _____ State _____ ZIP _____

Home phone _____ Work phone _____

Date of birth _____ Age _____ Gender: __ Male __ Female

Ethnicity: __ White __ Hispanic __ African American __ Asian __ Other _____

School _____ Grade _____

Emergency contact _____ Phone _____

Please list all members of your household:

Name	Sex	Age	Relationship to applicant

Application Questions

Please answer all of the following questions as completely as possible. If more space is needed, use an extra sheet of paper or write on the back of this page.

1. Why do you/your child want to participate in a mentoring program?

2. What are your expectations for the Cross-Age Mentoring Program (CAMP)?

3. Is your child available to meet with a mentor eight hours per month (two hours a week after school) for a minimum of one year? Please explain any particular scheduling issues.

4. Is your child willing to attend an initial mentee training session and two training sessions per year after being matched?

5. Describe your child's school performance including grades, homework, attendance, behaviors, etc.

6. Does your child have friends? Please describe his/her friendships.

7. Is your child currently having any problems either at home or school?

8. Has your child experienced any traumatic events (i.e., death in the family, abuse, divorce)? If yes, please provide details.

9. Provide any additional background information that may be helpful to CAMP in matching your son/daughter with an appropriate mentor.

Medical History

Name of primary care physician _____ Phone _____

Medical insurance provider _____

Policy number _____ Phone _____

Does your son/daughter have any physical problems or limitations?

Is your son/daughter currently receiving treatment for any medical issues?

Is he/she currently on any type of medication? If so, please specify.

Does your son/daughter have any known allergies or adverse reactions to medications? If yes, please describe them below:

Does your son/daughter have any emotional issues or problems right now?

Is your son or daughter currently seeing a counselor or therapist?

Therapist's name: _____

Please read this carefully before signing

This application is intended as a means of informing and gaining the consent of the parent/guardian to allow their son/daughter to participate in CAMP. After receiving this completed application from you, we will evaluate the information and send you a letter letting you know if your child has been accepted into the mentoring program. Much of the information you supply in this application packet will be used to match your child with an appropriate mentor. Therefore, the mentoring staff may, at times, need to access and share this information with prospective mentors and other parties when it is in the best interest of the match. However, we do not reveal names until there is an initial interest from the mentee, parent/guardian, and mentor based first upon anonymous information provided about each other.

Please initial each of the following

_____ I give my informed consent and permission for my child to participate in the CAMP and its related activities.

_____ I agree to have my child follow all mentoring program guidelines and understand that any violation on my child's part may result in suspension and/or termination of the mentoring relationship.

_____ I hereby acknowledge that my child can be transported by CAMP staff or representatives while participating in the CAMP, and that such transportation is voluntary and at his/her own risk.

_____ I release the CAMP of all liability of injury, death, or other damages to me, my child, family, estate, heirs, or assigns that may result from his/her participation in the program, including but not limited to transportation, and hold harmless any CAMP mentor, program staff, or other representatives, both collectively and individually, of any injury, physical or emotional, other than where gross negligence has been determined.

_____ (optional) I agree to allow CAMP to use any photographic image of my child taken while participating in the mentoring program. These images may be used in promotions or other related marketing materials.

I understand I must return all of the following completed items along with this application, and that any incomplete information will result in the delay of this application being processed:

• Contact and Information Release Form

• Interest Survey Form

By signing below, I attest to the truthfulness of all information listed on this application and agree to all the above terms and conditions.

Signature _____ Date _____

Please return or mail this application to:

Mentee Referral Form

Youth's name _____

Age _____ Grade _____

School _____

Requested by _____

Position _____ Phone _____

The child is being referred for assistance in the following areas (circle all that apply):

Academic Issues	Behavioral Issues	Delinquency	Vocational Training
Self-Esteem	Study Habits	Social Skills	Peer Relationships
Family Issues	Special Needs	Attitude	Other, specify:

Why do you feel this youth might benefit from a mentor?

What particular interests, either in school or out, do you know of that the child has?

What strategies/learning models might be effective for a mentor working with this youth?

On a scale of 1–10 (10 being highest) rate the student's level of:

_____ Academic performance   _____ Communication skills

_____ Social skills   _____ Attitude about school/education

_____ Self-esteem   _____ Peer relations

_____ Family support

With what specific academic subjects, if any, does the student need assistance?

Additional comments:

Record-Keeping Policy Guidelines

A record-keeping policy defines who is responsible for keeping records of mentor and mentee applicants and describes the type of filing system necessary to maintain and update these records.

A record-keeping policy is important because it provides clear direction to the coordinator on how to document and store records of the screening and matching process. A record-keeping policy helps reduce program liability by ensuring that all information is kept confidential and is treated consistently, and it helps increase program effectiveness by providing a system for efficiently tracking applicants and monitoring matches. The record-keeping policy should also outline how and when information is to be destroyed.

Key development questions

- Who is responsible for creating and maintaining program records?
- What types of information should be documented?
- Do you have specific forms for tracking applicants and monitoring matches?
- Do you have a system in place for maintaining secure and confidential records of active program participants?
- Do you have a secure and confidential archival system for maintaining records of past program participants?
- When and how do you destroy records?
- Are electronic data stored securely and backed up periodically? If so, by whom and how often?

Sample record-keeping policy

Board approval date _____ Revision date _____

It is the policy of the Cross-Age Peer Mentoring Program (CAMP) that each step of the mentoring application and match process be documented by creating a case file for each potential mentor and mentee. All forms for managing mentor and mentee case files are included within the procedures section of this manual.

All records are to be kept confidential and are to be covered by the conditions outlined in the confidentiality policy. Archival records or those records of past applicants and participants will be maintained and kept confidential for a period of seven years after the close of their participation in the program. After seven years, the records will be shredded and discarded with approval from the executive director and destroyed only by approved individuals.

The program coordinator must keep stringent records of all program activities, utilizing approved forms. All files should be regularly maintained and updated within an electronic database and/ or hard copy filing system. The creation of new forms or the revision of existing forms must be documented and kept within the policy and procedure manual.

Mandatory Reporting of Child Abuse and Neglect Procedure Content

This procedure determines the steps required to comply with the mandatory reporting of child abuse and neglect as required by your state (and your corresponding mandatory reporting policy). It is critical that all staff, agency representatives, and volunteers or mentors fully understand what constitutes child abuse and neglect in your state and how they must report it.

In developing this procedure for your program, you must refer to your state's statutes regarding child abuse and neglect, and confer with your executive director, board of directors, legal counsel, and any risk management advisers. Your program must determine the time frame within which reporting must occur from the time it is suspected, what records are kept and where, with whom they are shared, and who must report the suspected occurrence to state authorities. This procedure must be carefully thought out, including how to process these reports during nonworking hours.

What to include (examples follow):

__ Mandatory Reporting of Child Abuse and Neglect Procedure Recommendations

__ Child Abuse and Neglect Report Form

Mandatory Reporting of Child Abuse and Neglect Procedure Recommendations

Note: Any instructions, agencies, or statutes noted within this example procedures are purely fictional and are not meant to portray necessary steps that any agency or program should or must follow! Please consult your agency's legal counsel and state statutes for guidance in developing a tailored Mandatory Reporting procedure for your program.

Board approval date _____   Revision date _____

All staff, agency representatives, and volunteers must adhere to the following mandatory reporting procedures.

Suspected child abuse or neglect

1. All suspected incidents of child abuse or neglect, recent or otherwise, must be reported to the program coordinator immediately, the same day if possible.

2. The program coordinator must fill out the Child Abuse and Neglect Report form detailing critical information about the alleged incident of abuse or neglect. Once completed and reported, this form will be kept in the mentee's file folder.

3. The program coordinator must then file a report with the state Department of Children and Family Services (DCFS) within 24 hours per state statute.

4. If knowledge of the suspected abuse or neglect occurs during nonbusiness hours, the mentor must 1) contact the agency crisis staff on beeper, or 2) make the report to the local community abuse hotline or directly to children's protective services. The mentor must first attempt to contact agency/program staff. If unable to do so at the time, he/she must file a report with the program coordinator by noon the next business day. The program coordinator must follow steps 1 and 2 above and follow up with the DCFS to ensure the report was adequately made by the mentor.

5. In some cases, the DCFS may require the mentor to be interviewed or make contact with them directly. In such cases, the program coordinator will accompany the mentor as allowed by DCFS.

Suspected child abuse or neglect by program staff or volunteers

1. The same procedures outlined above will be followed for any suspected child abuse and neglect by any staff person, program representative, or volunteer.

2. In addition, the alleged abuser will be investigated by New Insights executive staff and board members.

3. During such an investigation, the alleged abuser will be immediately restricted from contact with youth, placed on employment probation, terminated, or suspended from participation in the program.

4. In the case of suspicion of a mentor, the parent/guardian will be immediately informed of the suspicion.

Training

1. All program staff, agency representatives, and volunteers must be trained on state statutes of child abuse and neglect laws, and the agency's mandatory reporting policy and procedures prior to working with youth or participating in the Cross–age Mentoring Program (CAMP).

2. Reporting of child abuse and neglect is mandated by the training policy and procedure and is included as a required topic in the training curriculum outline for both mentors and mentees.

Sample Child Abuse and Neglect Report Form

Date _____

Person making report to CAMP _____

Relationship to child _____

Reported to (DCFS staff name) _____ Date _____

Name of child _____ Age _____

Address _____

City _____ State _____ ZIP _____

Phone _____

Parent/guardian _____

Relationship to child _____

Person suspected of abuse or neglect _____

Relationship to the child _____

Describe suspected abuse or neglect; include the nature and extent of the current injury, neglect, or sexual abuse to the child in question:

Describe, if known, the circumstances leading to the suspicion that the child is a victim of abuse or neglect. Describe, if known, any previous injuries, sexual abuse, or neglect experienced by this child or other children in this family situation and any previous action taken, if any.

Unacceptable Behavior Policy

It is understood that there may be moments when the mentor or mentee's behavior is unacceptable. Ultimately, the parent is responsible for the child's discipline. However, it is CAMP's policy that the following guidelines are to be used if the parent is not around to assume the responsibility for the child's behavior. CAMP staff must inform the parent about the steps they took and why they took them.

- CAMP staff and mentors never physically discipline a mentee
- CAMP staff never use abusive language
- Ultimatums are not given as a result of unacceptable behavior
- CAMP staff and mentors explain to their mentee why certain behaviors are found unacceptable
- CAMP staff and mentors explain their concerns to mentors/mentee
- On rare occasions, the mentee may need to be taken home because of unacceptable behavior

Before taking this action, tell him/her what you are doing and why you made the decision. Taking your mentee back home because of his/her behavior doesn't necessarily mean the match (relationship) has ended. Before you leave make sure the child understands he/she will see you again and that you are not using his/her behavior as a pretext to abandon the relationship.

(Adapted from MENTOR toolkit, page 138)

Confidentiality Policy

All mentors/volunteers must complete the following confidentiality agreement.

All the information you are told about your student is confidential and sharing that information with others is prohibited. However, you are required to report certain things. Do promise a student that you will keep confidential information secret. Tell the student that he/she is free to share confidential information with you but that you are required to report certain things. It is critical, not only for the welfare of the student, but also to protect yourself that you adhere to these exceptions:

1. If a student confides that he or she is the victim of sexual, emotional, or physical abuse, you must notify _____(program coordinator) immediately.

Note on your calendar when this information was reported and to whom it was given. Remember, this information is extremely personal and capable of damaging lives, so do not share it with anyone except the appropriate authorities.

2. If a student tells you about his/her involvement in any illegal activity you must tell _____ (program coordinator) immediately. Again, note on your calendar when this information was reported and to whom it was given.

Summary

These procedures are designed to protect the students from harm and to prevent even the appearance of impropriety on the part of (name of program) and its participating mentors, volunteers and students. One accusation could, at the very least, seriously damage of those participating and endanger (name of program).

Please know that we appreciate your participation in the (name of program) and that we appreciate your adherence to these procedures. If you have any questions, please call (name of program) at (phone number).

I have read, understand and agree to strictly abide by the (name of program) Mentor/Volunteer Procedures. I understand that failure to adhere to these procedures may result in my removal from participation in the program.

Signature _____ Printed name _____

Date _____

Courtesy of Florida Governor's Mentoring Initiative, Mentor Tool Kit for Faith-Based Organizations (from MENTOR toolkit, page 141)

Program Participation Continuation Form

Dear CAMP mentee parent/guardian:

For the past year, your child has participated in CAMP. As the end of the year approaches and the program nears an end, we would like to extend our sincere thanks and appreciation for supporting your child's participation.

Additionally, we would like to invite your child to continue his/her participation in CAMP. As has been explained, CAMP includes a summer component. We are requesting that you let us know whether or not your child will be participating in either the CAMP summer program or the annual mentoring program beginning again in the fall. Your prompt response will allow us to properly plan for both components of CAMP. Please return the form below as soon as possible.

We hope that your child will continue to participate in CAMP, but we understand that other barriers might impede attendance. We thank you again for your service.

Child's name _____

Please mark the following:

___ Yes, my child will be participating in the CAMP summer program.

___ Yes, my child will be participating in the annual mentoring program beginning in the fall.

___ No, my child will no longer be participating in CAMP.

Signature _____

Program Evaluation Consent Form

9/13/00

Dear Parent,

This is a letter asking for your permission to allow your child to serve as either a mentor to a child in the middle or elementary school or to be a mentee in the program, and to participate in the evaluation of the mentoring program by completing a survey twice each year and allowing our program access to your child's academic records to access grades, behavior, and attendance information. This information will be used only for the purpose of evaluating the program, and any results that are made available to the public will not identify any youth who participated in the program or evaluation.

As a part of our efforts to help students achieve in school and become successful adults, we developed a cross-age afterschool mentoring program. In this mentoring program, high school students are paired with middle or elementary school mentees, with whom they meet on school grounds once a week after school, during four scheduled SuperSaturdays, and for one week during summer. Mentors are asked to commit to working with their mentee in this way for one year, to participate in monthly supervisions at school, to attend occasional field trips on Saturdays (e.g., Children's Museum), and commit to working one afternoon a week for a year.

This is a consent form requesting your permission to enroll your child in this program. There are a limited number of program places each year, so some students will be placed on a wait list and will be included in the evaluation of the program. If placed on the wait list, your child will be given priority over new applicants in the coming school year. This increases the likelihood that your child can participate in the program.

We ask your permission to allow us to collect questionnaires from your child about social skills, school attitude and motivation, behaviors in school, and self-esteem; and periodically to view your child's school records as part of our research to evaluate the program's effectiveness. From the school records, we will only collect information on your child's grades, behavior referrals, and attendance.

The questionnaires will not become part of your child's school record, and will not be provided to teachers or school administrators in any way that would identify your child. This information is confidential, and will be kept in a locked file cabinet for seven years and then destroyed. Only individuals working on the evaluation will be given access to the data, and once your child's information is entered into the computer file, his or her name will be blacked out of forms that are stored in these locked file cabinets.

It is important that we collect this information so that we can make sure the program is effective in helping children succeed in school. However, if you do not wish for your child to participate in the program or to be part of the evaluation, he or she does not have to. Students also may discontinue participation at any time. Students will not be penalized or lose privileges at school if they decline to participate.

We foresee no risks to your child's participation in the program or program evaluation, and believe that being involved can be one of the most rewarding experiences during your child's school years. We hope you will allow your child to participate and will help and encourage her or him to attend both afterschool meetings and SuperSaturday events four times during the school year.

Please note, mentors are not encouraged to meet with mentees outside of these supervised meetings, but are encouraged to write, call, or e-mail their mentees. Training and supervision will be provided to all mentors and tutors.

By signing this permission form, I (sign name)_____, agree to allow the Project Coordinator of CAMP to include my child _____ as a mentor/mentee or as part of the wait list group (who serve as a comparison group this year) in order to be a part of the evaluation. I understand I may discontinue my child's participation any time without penalty to her or him and that all mentors will receive training and supervision.

I (sign name)_____, agree to allow the Project Coordinator of CAMP and members of the evaluation team to collect questionnaires twice a year from my child _____.

I (sign name)_____, agree to allow the Project Coordinator of CAMP to view my child's files for their program evaluation and research.

Please sign and return this form to the school. The survey measures are available in the school's main office for you to view. If you have any questions about the surveys, how they will be used, or about the mentoring program or research, please call the Project Coordinator of CAMP or the principal. Thank you.

Appendix C. Checklists for Formative Evaluation

Touching Base 3-2-1 Activity Mentor Instruction Sheet

Each person shares **three** things that happened in the past week (or month) that were good. Good things can be successes the person experienced, a connection that was strengthened (e.g., to a friend, teacher, sibling, or classmates), or way in which they had fun at school or outside of school. This is intended to help one another learn what is unique, special, and interesting about their life.

Example: Mentor: "I found out that after working really hard, I was able to earn an A on the final exam, and that helped me earn a solid B in a class I was previously struggling in." Or, "Last weekend I got to go see my dad. I don't see him often since my parents' divorce, and sometimes it's weird when we get together (because we have not seen each other in a while); but this time, it was really fun."

Each person shares **two** things that happened in the week (or month) that were experienced as bad things. Bad things might be failures or challenges the person has not yet overcome, a disconnection that happened (e.g., between oneself and a friend, parent, teacher, or classmate), or some difficult experience (e.g., loss of a friend or family member).

Each person shares **one** thing the person plans to do to make more good things happen in his life or how the person plans to deal with problems in the coming week.

Explain the rationale—it is a quick way to find out what has gone on each other's life since the last meeting, and to capture both the highs and the lows of the prior week. It also provides a chance for either the mentor or the mentee to learn whether or not the other has a pressing problem or issue that needs to be addressed, one that might otherwise interfere with the mentor or mentee's ability to fully engage in the activity.

3-2-1 Relationship Reflections (Quarterly) Mentor Instruction Sheet

- Each person names **three** things they really like about the other person, three special times they had together; or three things they really enjoyed doing together.

- Each person shares **two** things about the other person, or their time together, that made it hard to connect.

- Each person shares **one** thing that they will do differently in this or their next relationship, or one hope they have for the other person or for their relationship.

This Relationship Reflection happens every quarter (rather than weekly) as relationships grow through time.

Mentor and mentee share with the each other what they have done together that built connectedness between them and what has interfered with connectedness (such as disrupted trust or decreased feelings of safety that resulted in one person feeling unsupported, or something that made one person not want to be with the other). Then, each should express one idea about a change they can make to improve their relationship now, or in the future.

Just as with the Touching Base 3-2-1 Activity this information should be written down, so that a "relationship history" is recorded over time. This relationship history—the writing of "their story" together—will come in very handy when playing the Newly Matched Game (to be discussed the next week), and when reflecting on their time together, at the end of the school year, when each relationship is closed or "terminated."

3-2-1 Touching Base Activity (Weekly) Summary Form

Name _____ Date _____

Three good things that happened to me last week were:

Two bad things that happened to me last week were:

One thing I plan to do differently to make more good things happen to me or to improve a difficult situation that is happening to me is:

Daily Activity Reflection: Mentee

Mentors and mentees should spend a few moments following the Core Activity to offer a brief "reflection" on what they thought of the activity and the match. Remember to provide this to program staff before leaving.

"For the record … " (Mentee)

Date _____

Activity _____

I thought this activity was (circle):

GREAT! LOTS OF FUN   IT WAS OKAY   NOT MUCH FUN

      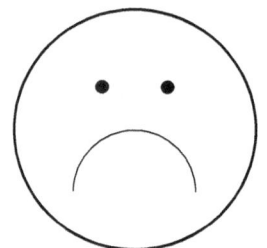

Something I liked about this activity (or time with my mentor):

Something I didn't like so much:

Daily Activity Reflection: Mentor

Mentors and mentees should spend a few moments following the Core Activity to offer a brief "reflection" on what they thought of the activity and the match. Remember to provide this to program staff before leaving.

"For the record …" (Mentor)

Date _____

Activity _____

I thought this activity was (circle):

AWESOME! LOTS OF FUN!   WE WORKED TOGETHER   THERE WERE SOME
WE CONNECTED!   AND GOT THE JOB DONE   CHALLENGES!

  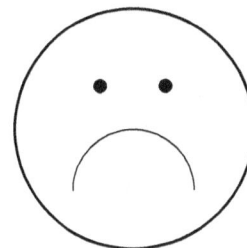

What I liked about today's activity:

Something positive happened with my mentee:

Things that were a challenge:

3-2-1 Relationship Reflection: (Quarterly) Record

Name _____ Date _____

Three things I like about my mentor/mentee, or three special times we had together so far this year; or three things I really enjoyed doing together are:

Two things about the my mentor/mentee or about our time together that made it hard to connect sometimes were:

One thing that I will do differently in my relationship this year or next year in my relationship, or one hope I have for my mentee/mentor or our relationship is:

Appendix D. Data Collection

Some Tips for Collecting Evaluation Data

Parent surveys

Parents are most eager to complete surveys when they think it will improve their children's chances of getting into or staying in a program. So, surveys at admission (spring the year prior) and at the end of year (the following spring), when we collect consent to participate for a second year, provide the best response rates.

Parents can report in a biased manner (being overly positive or overly negative). Depending on how the surveys are provided (or "explained") to parents, and partly as a response to what they understand the program to be about (e.g., for all kids, "troubled kids") and how competitive they think admission to the program may be, some will over report problems or try to cast their child as a star child. Asking for an honest assessment of their child's behavior and attitudes over the past several months is essential to collecting useful data.

For example: "In order to evaluate our school-based programs, we create a picture of all youth in the program. The picture is an average of all children's scores, and no child's individual scores will be included in records or provided to teachers or other school administrators. Scores will not be used to determine students' future participation in any programs. But for the evaluation to be useful, we need very honest and accurate data. Please answer the following questions based on what your child has said or how your child has acted in the past two months."

Teacher surveys

Teachers are often unwilling or unable to provide survey descriptions of youth who have only been in their classes a few weeks, so we don't usually collect surveys in the fall from teachers. But, when using the class cohort design, you will want to enter classes in the fall and spring to survey the students. If you just survey teachers in the spring, they will feel more comfortable assessing their students and you have time to develop a collaborative relationship with them.

It rarely hurts and can sometimes help to tape a candy or add a handwritten, personal note thanking the teacher ahead of time for completing the survey. When administrators are somehow made aware of how helpful cooperating teachers are, over time this too can increase participation and compliance when surveying.

Teachers have limited time. Keeping the survey to one page or less is ideal. We suggest only assessing the connectedness behaviors and the problem behaviors.

Youth surveys

Both mentors and mentees can be surveyed in small groups. The setting should be quiet (e.g., a library or emptied cafeteria) and the kids should be spaced apart. This will help them take the survey seriously.

If the mentees are surveyed separately, they should be told that the surveys will not be used to place kids in the program or matched with mentors, but that the usefulness of the evaluation depends on their honesty. Let the youth know that no youth survey will be shared with anyone without the youth or youth's parental permission. Let them know the people who fund the program need to see the evaluation reports (average scores for the whole group) for them to continue funding the program, so honestly and completeness is essential.

If you use the cohort design, you might be able to survey prospective and current mentees alongside classmates, who are serving as the comparison group. If you have buy in from the school to let you survey all the youth in the grades you serve with your program, the surveying will be less apparently related to CAMP. A larger pool also facilitates the mentee-comparison student matching (e.g., propensity score matching) or may be used to increase your overall sample size.

Survey administration with mentees and comparison youth

Fourth-graders are at the lower edge of having the readings skills and attention to complete surveys autonomously. For fourth-, fifth-, and sometimes sixth-graders, it can be useful to read the surveys aloud to the youth as they complete the surveys in groups. Room monitors (e.g., mentors from a different after school group) should float around the room and make sure the kids are staying focused and on the right questions.

The Hemingway Measure includes "negatively worded" items. This is great, if it serves its purpose, which is to avoid a response set (answering "strongly agree" to every question). But, if youth are not paying attention and engage in such patterned responding, the reliability of the scale will be lowered considerably. So, when reading the surveys, it can help to alter the tone of delivery of these items to be sure they are kept aware of the need to listen carefully and identify these items. Also, you can let students know ahead of time to look out for these.

"Students, as you complete the surveys pay close attention to sentences that are negatively phrased, like 'I never get along with my parents.' Look for words like never, seldom, and not, and make sure you don't assume every sentences measures a positive quality."

Most often, the surveys will be hand entered. If they are scanned using a scanner and scanning software, pencils are necessary. Otherwise, pen is fine.

Make sure youth put their name, age, sex, and other necessary information on the survey before turning it in. It can help to request this right after the instructions. For example, "Students, before you begin the survey, please make sure to enter your name, gender and age and any other information at the top of page."

Scoring Surveys

After data are collected from kids using paper surveys, the responses have to be translated into numbers to allow statistical analyses. (If the survey is done online, such as using SurveyMonkey, this option is already available; although you have to instruct the site to give you numerical output rather than the actual text response.)

There are two types of files that can be used to enter the surveys, Excel and SPSS (which stands for Statistical Package for the Social Sciences). Entering the data into an Excel file is fine, and the files can be accessed on several websites (see www.adolescentconnectedness.com and www.mentoringteens.com).

Each response is associated with a number. For the Hemingway subscales of adolescent connectedness, the scores range from 1 to 5.

Not at all true = 1
Not really true = 2
Sort of true = 3
True = 4
Very true = 5

Depending on what the surveys looks like, you may see these numbers on the form (as in the Scantron version of the form below), or you may just see the response alone (e.g., "Very true"). Either way, it is important to enter the number that youth has reported in the column for that item.

Please use this survey to tell us about yourself. Read each statement. MARK the number that best describes how true that statement is for you or how much you agree with it. If a statement is unclear to you, ask for an explanation. If it is still unclear, mark the "?".

"How TRUE about you is each sentence?"

	Not at all true	Not really true	Sort of true	True	Very true	? Unclear
(1) I like hanging out around where I live (like in my neighborhood).	①	②	③	④	⑤	⑦
(2) Spending time with friends is not so important to me.	①	②	③	④	⑤	⑦
(3) I can name 5 things that my friends like about me.	①	②	③	④	⑤	⑦
(4) My family has fun together.	①	②	③	④	⑤	⑦
(5) I have a lot of fun with my brother(s) or sister(s). (leave blank if you have none)	①	②	③	④	⑤	⑦
(6) I work hard at school.	①	②	③	④	⑤	⑦
(7) My classmates often bother me.	①	②	③	④	⑤	⑦
(8) I care what my teachers think of me.						

Helpful hint: Misentry of data can undermine an entire evaluation. To identify misentry, you can (as many data entry firms do) have the surveys entered twice. Then, compare the documents to see where discrepancies are, and return to the surveys to correct them. That way you can be sure your data were entered correctly. Both Word and Excel offer this function (I don't think SPSS does)—"compare documents"—and it can be very helpful.

After the data have been entered, it may be easiest to have someone else compute the scales and run the analyses. We've made this easier for them (and less costly for you) by providing the syntax in paper and digital form. That way, you can provide an evaluator or researcher the data file (your kids' data) along with the syntax for scoring the data, and the syntax for running the comparisons. They, they can help you interpret the findings.

Missing data

Before the evaluator can prepare the data, it is important to be sure there are no misentries, double-entries, or erroneously missing values. The double-entry method described above will help with all three of these problems, but the truly missing data also may need to be imputed. To impute means to use for missing responses the predicted scores of missing values estimated from responses on other items. Some statistical packages can do this, but not all. It is an "add-on" module for missing values in SPSS (which can cost several hundred dollars, so not everyone who owns it also has SPSS).

Depending on how subscales are computed, such as using SPSS, missing data may eliminate an entire case (person). The main reason is that if a single item is missing for a subscale (and most subscales, like "Connectedness to school" have 5), and a formula is used to create the subscale that requires all subscale items (e.g., "Hem4 + Hem 14 + Hem 24 + Hem 34/4") it may render the subscale "missing." So, if the statistical program used to compute the subscale scores uses a "listwise deletion method," this should be changed.

In the syntax provided, the subscales are computed with all available items. This is not ideal, and it would be preferable to impute missing values before computing subscales, but give the complexity of this task, we know not all will undertake missing data imputation. So discuss missing data with your evaluator, and do your best to get complete data from everyone who completes your surveys.

Recoded negatively worded items in data

The first thing the evaluator does (once she is sure there are no misentered data, such as 55 for 5 or 6 for a 3 that can result from hand entered miskeying), is to recode the negatively worded items. See item #7 in the figure above. This is a negatively worded item on peer connectedness. It has to be reversed before it can be pooled or averaged into a subscale score with the other items on that subscale which are all positively worded. So, if a child reports a 1 ("Not at all true"), then the computer has to change it to a 5 ("Very true"). If the child enters a 4, that has to be changed to a 2. This is done with the RECODE command in the syntax. For the Hemingway subscales, the syntax looks like this:

```
RECODE
VHemA2 VHemA7 VHemA13 VHemA18 VHemA26 VHemA30 VHemA34 VHemA45
VHemA51 VHemA55
(1=5) (2=4) (4=2) (5=1).
EXECUTE.
```

This recode syntax above shows that variable (V) on the Hemingway: Adolescent Connectedness Scale (HemA) for survey numbers 2, 7, 13, 18...55 are all recoded. Most of the Hemingway scales are typically highly reliable, suggesting the construct assessed by each of the sentences is responded to consistent with the construct captured by the other items. Connectedness to Reading is one of these. Connectedness to Peers subscale items, however, are sometimes less reliable if the items are not consistent culturally or developmentally with the way a child views relationships with classmates (see Karcher & Sass, 2010). But, it also can yield a less-than-ideal reliability score partly as a function of the inclusion of the negatively worded items. (This is why some people don't include them in their surveys—but they run the risk of participants engaging in a "response set" which ultimately leads the subscales to be more highly intercorrelated than is true in real life. So, their subscales may be reliable, but they lack discriminant validity and thus utility.)

Reliability estimates

The second thing the evaluator does before running any analyses is look at the reliability of the items. The steps for this too are provided in the accompanying syntax for SPSS. Reliability for these subscales is estimated using "Cronbach's Alpha coefficient for internal consistency." You probably have a problem with survey administration (e.g., kids were goofing around and not paying attention) if this falls near or below .60 on any scale; in which case, you probably don't want to include that scale in your analyses—it just adds too much error into analyses and reduces your "power"—ability to find program effects that truly exist.

Here is an illustration of the kind of information that is provided by SPSS for each scale in response to the reliability syntax.

The syntax requesting the interitem reliability coefficient (alpha) reads:

```
RELIABILITY
/VARIABLES = VHemA7 VHemA17 VHemA27 VHemA37 VHemA47 VHemA57
/FORMAT = NOLABELS
/SCALE(ALPHA) = ALL/MODEL = ALPHA
/STATISTICS = DESCRIPTIVE SCALE
/SUMMARY = TOTAL.
```

The output provides descriptive information, the reliability estimate, information each item (its mean and standard deviation), and the reliability of the scale with each item singly deleted. The first information tells how many missing values there were and how many complete cases there were. In the example output below, there were 224 cases (84% of the sample) which were used because there were missing data for 44 kids. The alpha coefficient was low, .625. This means the correlation among all of the items was .625 leaving .375% of the variability among the items unaccounted for. But you can see that the negatively worded item lowered the reliability down from .70 (what it would have been without item 7, which is negatively worded), which is adequate, to .625, which is poor. In this case, we would not compute the scale using the negatively worded item.

Whether or not to drop the negatively worded item when computing subscales

In most cases, including this one, however, we don't recommend deleting these items. Not only does it change the scale (so validity estimates from prior research on the scale no longer apply), but it changes the scale. In prior research, we've found keeping the item in when computing the average subscale mean—as long as it is not negatively correlated with the other items (and does not decrease the reliability more than 10% or push it below. Alpha = .60)—is better and provides more accurate estimates than omitting it.

When an item on a scale is negatively correlated with other items

Negative correlations typically mean either (a) you have not recoded the negative items, or (b) the responders really were not paying very good attention during the survey. When the correlations are negative, it may be necessary to compute the reliabilities without the negatively worded items. But if you do this on one administration (e.g., the pretest), you need to do it on other administrations (e.g., the posttest), otherwise you will be comparing different scales.

```
TITLE   "Hemingway Adolescent Version 5.5 Reliability Estimate".
```

» Hemingway Adolescent Version 5.5 Reliability Estimate

```
SUBTITLE Subscale Below Entitled:  Connectedness to Peers'.
```

» Hemingway Adolescent Version 5.5 Reliability Estimate
  Subscale Below Entitled: Connectedness to Peers'

```
RELIABILITY
 /VARIABLES=VHemA7 VHemA17 VHemA27 VHemA37 VHemA47 VHemA57
 /FORMAT=NOLABELS
 /SCALE(ALPHA)=ALL/MODEL=ALPHA
 /STATISTICS=DESCRIPTIVE SCALE
 /SUMMARY=TOTAL .
```

Reliability

```
[DataSet1] /Users/michaelkarcher/Desktop/Curtis_Data6_1_11.sav
```

Scale: ALPHA

Case Processing Summary

		N	%
Cases	Valid	224	83.6
	Excluded[a]	44	16.4
	Total	268	100.0

a. Listwise deletion based on all variables in the procedure.

Reliability Statistics

Cronbach's Alpha	N of Items
.625	6

Item Statistics

	Mean	Std. Deviation	N
VHemA7	3.53	1.159	224
VHemA17	3.21	.891	224
VHemA27	3.21	.911	224
VHemA37	3.38	.976	224
VHemA47	3.46	.970	224
VHemA57	3.19	1.278	224

Item-Total Statistics

	Scale Mean if Item Deleted	Scale Variance if Item Deleted	Corrected Item-Total Correlation	Cronbach's Alpha if Item Deleted
VHemA7	16.45	11.755	.059	.702
VHemA17	16.77	10.538	.386	.574
VHemA27	16.77	10.439	.390	.572
VHemA37	16.60	9.568	.504	.526
VHemA47	16.51	9.758	.473	.538
VHemA57	16.79	8.696	.429	.551

Computing subscales

Once that data have been cleaned, inspected for misentry or missing data, and reliability has been checked and deemed sufficient, then it is time to compute the subscales and run the analyses. The COMPUTE syntax will compute the subscales. In the syntax provided, it will compute the mean score for the items available in a subscale. If an item is missing, it will be left out. (Note, this is not always the case in SPSS, and if evaluators do not use the command "MEAN(var1, var2 ...)" but instead type in the formula, such as "(var1+var2+var3)/3", then any missing item will result in a missing subscale estimate.) The only problem with this is that if it is the negative item that is missing, the subscale score will be slightly higher than otherwise for the individual who did not complete the negatively worded item. If a positively worded item is left out, the subscale score may be slightly lower than otherwise. Usually, this is not a big problem.

When surveys can't be completed fully

When it really causes a problem is when an individual completes only half of the survey, and as a result the ratio of negative to positively worded items is particularly high. For example, if a youth only completes the first 15 items on the Hemingway survey, the Connectedness to Peers subscale would be based only on two items (reflect the average of), items 7 and 17, and 7 was negatively worded. So that youth will have a lower connectedness to peers subscale score than is true.[2] The REAL problem emerges, however, when something happens (such as the survey session being interrupted) so that all of the youth in a survey session have such low, biased scores. This can cause a problem. So, think about whether to use partially completed surveys or data from youth whose session was interrupted.

---

2 The reason for this is even after recoding variables, there is a negativity bias in the United States, such that Americans don't like to be as negative about themselves as they are positive. So, even if it is the same sentence reversed, a youth might give a 5 (always true) to the sentence, "All of my friends like me a lot," but only give a 2 (not really true) if it is worded negatively: "None of my friends like me a lot." So the recode gives a 4 rather than a 5 because of this negativity bias.

Conducting Statistical Analyses

Make sure "Skew and Kurtosis" are not too high before conducting analyses

Once the scales are computed, it is useful to assess their skew and kurtosis using the "Descriptives" option in SPSS, and this will indicate whether or not the scales are appropriate to use in statistical analyses that assume a normal distribution—balanced bell-shaped curve. If one side of the distribution (bell curve) has a longer tail than the other (skew) or if the bell is not normal in its peak but is more flat or extremely peaked, then statistical adjustments need to be conducted to try to achieve a more normal distribution.

Assuming the data are appropriate for analyses, the goal, then is to compare the means of the two groups to see if the youth who are a given age who participated in the program have higher scores (on positive scales like connectedness and self-esteem) than similarly aged youth who have not been in the program (your "counterfactual").

Whether or not to run the analyses yet: How big is your sample?

Earlier we discussed the problem of statistical significance testing given the typical sample sizes that mentoring programs have, such as between 50–60 participants at a time. I suggested, therefore, that several years of data be collected to achieve a sample size of 300 mentees and another 300 comparison kids (or at least 225 comparison kids). This is the best way to achieve adequate statistical power to reduce the likelihood of finding a program effect if indeed the program has one. This estimate of several hundred mentees is given the expected effect size ($d = .20$, or a 1/5 standard deviation difference in group means) and conventions regarding the significance level to be used (i.e., $p < .05$, which refers to the probability of less than 1/20 of finding an effect "this large or larger" in a population wherein no real group differences are present). Remember, once you run your analyses, you have to accept the results, and you want the cards to be stacked in your favor.

Don't forget covariates

The other way we increase statistical power (which is almost always a good thing to do) is to include "covariates" in our analyses. Covariates are variables that are correlated with our outcome measures and which may or may not be associated with program participation. In essence, every construct we assess (misbehavior, social interest, empathy, connectedness, self-esteem) has many "causes." There are also lots of between-group differences on such constructs other than whether or not someone was mentored. You want to know (and are testing with your analyses) whether the variability in outcomes associated with program participation is large relative to the remaining, unexplained error. So any error you can remove from the "unexplained error" should increase the ratio of explained to unexplained error (and increase power). You want to use covariates to explain variability in that outcome construct that is irrelevant to the program and that just adds error to our analyses (or clouds our ability to estimate true between group, treatment differences).

Include the pretest score as a covariate

The biggest covariate is the person's prior score on the same variable. Knowing what a score was on a given construct one year prior will usually explain 25 to 50 percent of the variance in the score a year later. This variability also clouds our interpretation of treatment effects. So, we want to include covariates in our analyses, so that any variability (unrelated or accidentally) related to our outcome is accounted for before we estimate our program effect. This covariate might be the pretest completed in the application phase the prior spring or at the start of the year.

The test statistic (and associated p-value)

The effect of the program will be, in essence, determined by a critical test statistic, which reflects the amount of explained and unexplained variability in our outcome of interest. After we remove considerable variability in the outcome of interest that is due to such covariates as the pretest score on that construct, age, gender, etc., the likelihood that the amount of variability in our outcome associated with program participation (being in the program or not) will reflect a statistically significant (i.e., relatively reliable and trustworthy) difference in group means. The p-value is the probability of finding a mean difference between mentored and unmentored kids as large as the one observed in our analyses if in fact there was no "true" difference in the groups. The p-value less than .05 says that if you ran the same analyses on the exact same kind of program 100 times, only 5 times in a 100 would you the observed this difference if it was not really true or real.

Analyses of covariance

What the analysis of covariance does is try to equate the two groups on the covariate buy adjusting the outcome accordingly. With analyses of covariance, we are asking, therefore, whether, after one has "controlled for" or explained away irrelevant variability in our outcomes that is due to nonprogram-related factors, is there a difference between those who did and did not participate in CAMP the year prior to completing that assessment.

Now, were we not to use analysis of covariance, we could use Excel pretty easily to compute mean differences. But analysis of covariance (i.e., including covariates) is a bit more complicated in Excel. There are ways to get around using SPSS, and only using Excel. But explaining them is beyond this chapter. For our purpose, we just want you to understand why we are collecting and using data in our analyses on such seemingly unrelated variables as age, gender, prior experience, etc. These covariates help us increase the likelihood we find effects, assuming our program has effects.

Appendix E. Evaluation

Elements of Program Implementation to Assess in Formative Evaluation

1. Fidelity:
    Recruitment
        Mentor Screening Scales
    Meet-and-Greet Event
    Afterschool
        Location
        Transportation
        Leadership
        Curriculum
        Materials
        1-2-3 (development ladder)
        3-2-1 (activity reflection)
    SuperSaturday
    Summer Event

2. Dosage:
    Attendance:
        Weekly afterschool
        Quarterly SuperSaturdays
            Youths
            Parents
        Annual summer program
    Percent of curricula used

3. Quality of delivery
        Mentor's nonverbal (mentor observation or mentee midyear survey)
            Warm, friendly, supportive
            Attentive
            Praising
        Mentors involve others
        Mentors encourage mentees
            To participate in activities
            To interact prosocially
        Share info and examples

4. Participant responsiveness
        Program stimulates interest
            of mentors
            of mentees

5. Distinctive content emphasizes
        Connectedness
        Perspective taking
        Social skills

6. Program reach
>   Mentee group includes
>> < 10% high-risk, school-referred youth
>> < 20% with high misbehavior scores
>> > 25% nonreferred, low risk
>
>   Mentors are high in
>> Attitudes towards youth (mentor application)
>> Social interest (mentor application)
>> Empathy (mentee midsurvey)
>
>   Few mentors
>> Work > 10 hours a week in a job
>> Participate in > 2 other activities

7. Program adaptations
>   Do:
>>> Reflect stakeholder input
>>> Discuss changes with stakeholders
>>> Adhere to goals of program
>>> Reflect connectedness training
>>> Foster perspective-taking skills
>
>   Do not:
>>> Stray from program theory or goals
>>> Allow students to associate with same-age peers frequently
>>> Deviate from supervised structure
>>> Vary time of program in ways that leave students unaccounted for

Checklist of Factors That Affect Implementation: To Review Before Running Program

I. Community-level factors

A. Prevention Theory and Research: The mentoring program is research/evidence-based, but has the support for the program been conveyed to stakeholders?

You've made the research available or shared it verbally with stakeholders, but do you have any evidence that the stakeholders are aware of expectable outcomes from youths' participation in the program? (Or, is there any evidence they prioritize other outcomes that the program does not target directly, and on which impacts are less likely?)

B. Politics: Does the program target goals shared by multiple stakeholders?

C. Funding: Does the program have a funding source (or, ideally, multiple dedicated sources of support)?

Is there a staff position covered by the district or the agency delivering the program, and has this person been relieved of other responsibilities so that she or he has sufficient time to conduct the program well?

Are there independent sources of funds for food, travel (field trips), staff positions, supplies, marketing (e.g., external: newsletters to parents; internal: t-shirts for mentors)?

D. Policy: Has a Memorandum of Understanding been established with the school to indicate the program's permission to use a specific school space, school resources (copier, phones, library, playing fields), busses (e.g., for after school transportation of youth), and staff time?

Has the sponsoring agency or school documented that the individual(s) responsible for operating the program will either be relieved of other duties (as noted above) or will be compensated in a clear, planned, and satisfactory manner to facilitate the ongoing involvement of program staff?

II. Provider characteristics

A. Perceived Need for CAMP: Is there evidence that CAMP is relevant to local needs, and has its relevance be conveyed (convincingly) to all stakeholders (administration, parents, teachers, and youth)? (see IA above as well)

B. Perceived Benefits of CAMP:

Have mentors been told about documented evidence that participation in CAMP is associated with improved academic connectedness and self-esteem[3], or that involvement in such programs is usually viewed positively by college admissions committees and employers?

Are parents aware that the mentors will be learning important social skills in order to effectively teach them to younger mentees?

Are parents and teachers aware of the impacts of CAMP participation on mentees' social skills and connectedness to school, teachers, and parents?[4]

---

3 Karcher, M.J. (2009). Increases in academic connectedness and self-esteem among high school students who serve as cross-age peer mentors. *Professional School Counseling, 12*(4), 292–299.

4 Karcher, M.J. (2005). The effects of developmental mentoring and High School mentors' attendance on their younger mentees' self-esteem, social skills, and connectedness. *Psychology in the Schools, 42*(1), 65–77.; Karcher, M.J., Davis, C.I., & Powell, B. (2002). The effects of developmental mentoring on connectedness and academic achievement. *School Community Journal, 12*(2), 36–50.

What is the extent to which the innovation will achieve benefits desired at the local level?

C. Mentor Self-efficacy:

Have you assessed the extent to which providers feel they will be able to do what is expected, and do you have a plan to review and respond to his information (i.e., the Mentor Efficacy intake survey)?

Have efforts been made to promote mentor-efficacy (e.g., through training)?

Have mentors been made aware that their feelings of mentor efficacy can shape the quality of their relationship with their mentees?[5]

Are there plans to conduct assessments of mentor efficacy at midyear to identify those mentors who may need additional support and individualized training?

D. Mentor Skill Proficiency: Do mentors possess the skills necessary for the implementation of CAMP—that is, to deliver the program content clearly and convincingly, enthusiastically and inclusively, and with appropriate interpersonal comments, gestures, and eye contact? (see delivery above)?

Have Program Coordinators or Lead Mentors made a plan for gathering feedback on activities from matches (e.g., Activity Reflection Cards with box and procedures) and for evaluative observations of mentors in action in order to identify strengths and weakness observed in mentors' approaches? Who will do it? When will they do it? How will skill be assessed?

Has a plan been drafted to provide feedback and steps for remediation if skills were observed to be lacking?

Is there a plan to conduct midyear evaluations of the mentees' connection with the mentors and program, review, and act on it for matches that are significantly low? If any mentee's ratings of "youth disappointment" is high, do you have a plan to ensure that mentors are not being rude, ignoring youth, or teasing them?

---

5 Karcher, M. J., Nakkula, M. J., & Harris, J. (2005). Developmental mentoring match characteristics: Correspondence between mentors' and mentees' assessments of relationship quality. *Journal of Primary Prevention, 26*(2), 93–110.

Implementation Checklist of Issues To Resolve or Address Before Starting Your CAMP

Safety plans:

- What has been planned and/or put in place to secure child safety?

- Will mentors drive to the school, will they carpool, and do all parents agree to this?

- Are policies in place to instruct youth as to where they are and are not to go?

- How has the possibility of deviancy training been addressed (see, Dodge, Dishion, & Lansford, 2006 for many examples), such as in the activities that are planned, the training that will be provided, the types of mentors and mentees who will be recruited, and in the options made available to them for free-time interactions?

Space: Have you secured spaces for the program that do not conflict with other programs?

Parents: Have you planned ways to involve more parents in weekend meetings, in a mentoring parent advisory committee, or in other ways?

Mentors' schedules:

- Being preventative, have you looked to see what competing extracurricular activities might emerge (that the mentors have not anticipated, but which you may) and conflict with program participation?

- Have you made accommodations so that mentors can remain in the program even when they are playing sports or other activities after school (e.g., either by asking the coach for one day off each week or by setting up a weekly lunch meeting between the mentor/mentees)?

Communication plan:

- Do you have plans (scheduled dates, distribution plan) for communication so that parents, teachers, and school staff (not just mentors and mentees) have advanced notice about scheduled meetings, trainings, evaluation assessments, etc.?

- Will this be done by mail, e-mail, what?

- Do all parents have access to the evaluation surveys, and know they have access?

- Have you determined your district's plan on data collection on students, and whether your program will require the use of parental consent forms for program evaluation?

Training:

- Have you determined and negotiated where trainings will take place and when?

- What plans have been made to inform mentors about the requirement of both initial and ongoing training?

- Are teachers aware that students may be pulled from class time to participate in the evaluation, and are they in agreement?

Mission clarity: To avoid "mission drift," consider what efforts you have made to explain the goals of the program and what types of kids are appropriate (and inappropriate) participants.

- Have you made efforts to communicate clearly to parents, mentors, and mentees about the nature of the program (e.g., that it is a social skills not an academic skills program) to avoid stigma that could undermine the program?

- Have you made clear to administrators, teachers, and parents early in the planning process that this is a "universal prevention program (for all kids) not an "indicated prevention program" (for kids at risk) to avoid stigma that could undermine the program?

- Do you know what you are going to say to the teacher, administrator, or parent who wants a particular high-risk (high needs, behaviorally problematic) kid in the program?

- Are you prepared to make referrals if parents want their children to get tutoring, homework help, counseling or other nonmentoring services?

Dishion, McCord, and Poulin (1999) presented research that increased the professional community's concerns about the potential negative effects of peer-based interventions for youth. Deviancy is the formal term for the process in which peers undercut the potential positive influences of conventional, adult-sanctioned activities and experiences by promoting, instead, authority undermining behaviors. They report that the youth most vulnerable to deviancy training are those more at risk for engaging in delinquent behavior. Explain to administrators, parents, and teachers that including youth most at risk for delinquent behaviors in CAMP may be the worst thing for those youth—not to mention its potential to limit the effectiveness of the program for others.

Finalize curriculum in advance: The curriculum needs to be ready before the program starts.

- In developing or adapting the curriculum, have you involved as many mentors (and other stakeholders) as possible, and kept CAMP goals in mind?

- Has it been completed by the end of the summer with activities and schedules and made available for teachers, parents and administrators to preview? (Most won't preview it, but if something goes wrong later, they had their chance.)

- Are the plans are as clear as possible (to help future staff take on the program development duties or reuse this curriculum in your absence in subsequent years)?.

Dissemination: Sometimes programs have been implemented locally in other schools.

- Did you get information from any recent program evaluations to the school (e.g., school board) and larger community (e.g., through newspapers and organizations) stakeholders.

- In your first year, did you report to these stakeholders what prior research has found?

- In subsequent years, did you get information from both formative and summative evaluations out to concerned stakeholders?

- Have you made efforts to keep the program high on everyone's radar screen?)(This is good PR and can also help in recruiting specific funds for projects, materials, field trips, etc.)

Participants roles: There are many players involved, and securing their involvement up front is essential.

- Who will plan, provide, and pay for snacks each day?

- Who will provide the program in the summer and on the SuperSaturday weekends?

- Who is the primary person responsible for the space that will be utilized after school (and do you have him or her on board)?

- Who has resources that may be needed for the program, including the free-time activities (such as librarians, cafeteria staff, coaches, groundskeepers), and do you have their approval for using these locations and any specific resources in these locations (e.g., books or computers in the library; balls from the gym; tables, napkins and utensils in the cafeteria, as well as wash basins, trash cans, and refrigerators).

- Because it is best to conduct early negotiations and establish clear communication to avoid frustration down the road, have you *established formal, documented Memoranda of Understanding detailing what others (and you) agree to provide, for how long, and under the direction, supervision, or support of whom?*

Clarify boundaries: It is important to decide whether or not mentors and mentees should have contact outside the program and if so under what conditions.

- How have you made clear to youth and their parents whether participants can e-mail each other or call each other, and if so, any parameters they must follow (e.g., no calls after 8 p.m.)?

- Have you made clear whether mentor and mentee can every meet outside the school and/or program context, and if so under what conditions this is appropriate (e.g., with one or the other's parental approval and supervision; with signed documentation by both mentors' and mentees' parents giving consent for such contact)? (Generally this is not advisable. But it is important to have a policy in place and approved by key stakeholders.)

CAMP compatibility: Does CAMP fit with the school's, community's, or agency's mission, priorities, and values? In what ways? Explain.

Questions to assess CAMP incompatibility:

- Would the school prefer a tutoring program, or does it insist on including a ratio of high to low risk mentees greater than 1:10?

- Will the school not contribute the resources (materials, financial, or staff necessary) to implement the program with fidelity—do they say they want the program but not act to ensure requests for resources are met or not complete the MOU?

CAMP adaptability: CAMP can be modified to fit provider preferences, organizational practices, and community needs, values, and cultural norms. While it is quite appropriate to create new curricula to address needs, cultural values, or goals specific to a given community or school, such changes would be evidence of *inadaptability* if doing so required the omission of any one key program element (e.g., SuperSaturdays, Curriculum or Meet-and-Greet).

- Adaptability parameters example of appropriateness: The Summer program may be adapted to be shorter or longer, provide more or less academic focus; but at least half of the mentors must be present, be focused on the kids (even other mentors' kids), and must help mentors provide a high quality delivery of program components (even academic).

- Adaptability parameters example of inappropriateness: Summer program, SuperSaturday, or after school program curricula are chosen or developed that (a) do not offer mentors a voice in creating and planning it, (b) that restrict mentors to simply symbolic appearances of ownership and partnership with adults; (c) that emphasize outcomes of content learned over the quality of the mentoring relationship; or (d) that adapt the configuration of the mentor-mentee relationship in ways the preclude consistent contact that affords opportunities for mentors and mentees to express empathy, praise, and attention to one another.

- Have program adaptations adhered to the core elements of the program?

- Are there any signs of inappropriate adaptations in play in your CAMP?

Data Collection Schedule

Early spring: Program establishment (Implementation evaluation data)

1. Program Coordinator checklist: a) Signed MOUs, b) program committee in place, c) contact person in each school active (Use Implementation checklist, in Appendix E)

2. Program Coordinator Contract for following year signed (position funded)

End of spring (Summative outcome evaluation data, Part 1)

3. Parent presurvey (mail home, Appendix F)

4. Teacher intake survey (deliver, Appendix F)

5. Mentor intake (collected at with application, Appendix A)

6. Mentee presurvey (collected in person in small group after receiving consent, Appendix F)

End of summer: Program startup checklist (Implementation evaluation data)

7. Program director checklist II: a) Curriculum completed, b) consent forms assembled, c) time and locations negotiated, d) budget (Use Implementation Checklist, in Appendix E)

Early winter: Program implementation data (Implementation evaluation data):

8. Mentor/mentee attendance

9. Degree of curriculum completed

10. Collection of Activity reflections (Appendix C)

11. Quarterly Relationship reflections (Appendix C)

Late winter/Early spring: Midyear surveys (Process evaluation data)

12. Parent midsurvey (adequacy of transportation; satisfaction with program; anticipated changes in child's life that may affect program participation or other information specific to your program)

13. Mentor midsurvey (adequacy of space; staff support, mentee mattering scale; and activity style checklist, Appendix F)

14. Mentee midsurvey: Goal/Growth-focus and Youth-Centered Relationship (10 items); feeling valued and motivated (12 items), and Mentor/Program Connectedness scale(Appendix F).

Late spring/Early summer (Formative and summative evaluation data, Part 2)

15. Parent postsurvey: Satisfaction with the program, youth interest in participation in following year, youth availability for summer program (if applicable), consent form(s), any anticipated changes in child's life that might affect participation in subsequent year (Appendix A)(or summer; Post surveys on child's connectedness, self-esteem. Appendix F)

16. Teacher postsurvey:

    16a. Teacher referral for new youth (Appendix A)

    16b. Assessment of student connectedness (school, teachers, reading, classmates, self-in-the-present, self-in-the-future, culturally different peers and class misbehavior (Appendix F)

17. Mentor postsurvey (connectedness, self-esteem, social interest, attitudes towards youth)

18. Mentee postsurvey

    18a. Satisfaction, Recommended changes, Interest in continued participation next year

    18b. Post survey (connectedness, self-esteem, problem behaviors, Appendix F)

19. Parent presurvey: Connectedness scales for parents enrolling child for next year

20. Teacher presurvey: Teacher ratings for students being enrolled for next year on student connectedness (school, teachers, reading, classmates, self-in-the-present, self-in-the-future, culturally different peers [if applicable]), class behavior (Herrera scale)(Appendix F)

Spring/summer: Program review (Implementation evaluation data)

21. Program director checklist III a) Review of MOU coverage (qual), b) program committee effectiveness (member attendance and Director-perceived helpfulness and teamwork), and c) contact person in each school availability and engagement), d) budget sufficiency, e) helpfulness of teachers/administration.

Summary of Which Measures Are Completed by Whom and When

Survey	Timing	Who completes	Scale
Intake			
		Parent	Connectedness
		Teacher	Connectedness
			Referral forms
		Mentor	MATY—Mentor Attitudes Towards Youth Scale
			Social Interest Scale
			Mentor Efficacy Scale
Presurvey	Early fall		
		Mentor	Hemingway Academic Connectedness Scales
			Self-Esteem Scales
			Training satisfaction survey
		Mentee	Hemingway Connectedness Scales
			Academic Self-Esteem Scales
			Misconduct scale
Weekly			
		Mentor	3-2-1 and Activity Reflection
		Mentee	3-2-1 and Activity Reflection
Mideval	Winter	Mentor	Staff Support
			Resources and Space
			Mentor efficacy
			Parental involvement
		Mentee	Youth-Centered Relationship
			Mentor/Program connection scales
			Feel valued by mentor scale
			Feel motivated by mentor scale
Postprogram	Late spring	Mentor	Hemingway Academic Connectedness
			Academic Self-Esteem Scales
			Program support
		Mentee	Hemingway Academic Connectedness
			Academic Self-Esteem Scales
			Misconduct scale
			Perceived support at school
		Teacher (post)	Hemingway Academic Connectedness
		Parent (post)	Hemingway Academic Connectedness

Appendix F. Forms for Analyses of Enabling and Distal Outcomes

Mentor Application Surveys

Crandall's Social Interest Scale (SIS)

Choose the description from each pair that best reflects what best explains who you would rather be. For each pair of personal characteristics or traits, select the trait that you value more highly. In making each choice, ask yourself which of the traits in that pair you would rather possess as one of your own characteristics. For example, the first pair is "imaginative—rational." If you had to make a choice, which would you rather be?

"I would rather be …"

Imaginative	or	rational	Neat	or	logical
Helpful	or	quick-witted	Forgiving	or	gentle
Neat	or	sympathetic	Efficient	or	respectful
Level-headed	or	efficient	Practical	or	self-confident
Intelligent	or	considerate	Capable	or	independent
Self-reliant	or	ambitious	Alert	or	cooperative
Respectful	or	original	Imaginative	or	helpful
Creative	or	sensible	Realistic	or	moral
Generous	or	individualistic	Considerate	or	wise
Responsible	or	original	Sympathetic	or	individualistic
Capable	or	tolerant	Ambitious	or	patient
Trustworthy	or	wise	Reasonable	or	quick-witted

Copyright 1975, by James E. Crandall, see also: http://www.psychbytes.com/Quizzes/Social%20Interest/Social%20Interest%20Scale.htm

Mentor Attitudes Toward Youth (MATY)

Root of each item: "How many kids in your community …"

Variable # (R=reversed)		None	Very Few	Some	Many	All or almost all	Response for item
1	Work hard at school	1	2	3	4	5	
2	Respect adults	1	2	3	4	5	
(R) 3	Are troublemakers	5	4	3	2	1	
4	Are fun to be around	1	2	3	4	5	
(R) 5	Expect things to be handed to them	5	4	3	2	1	
6	Try to do their best	1	2	3	4	5	
7	Are interested in learning	1	2	3	4	5	
						Sum of item responses	
						Divided by 7	÷7
						Average score	

Responses include 1 = none, 2 = very few, 3 = some, 4 = many, and 5 = all or almost all.
Scale calculated as a mean of seven items; higher score indicates more positive attitudes about youth aged 9–14 years.

(Herrera et al., 2007)

Mentor and Mentee Pre-Post Outcome Scale: Hemingway Measure of Adolescent Connectedness

(Also completed by mentors after they are accepted)

This instrument consists of items designed to measure the adolescents' degree of caring for and involvement in specific relationships and activities. The Measure of Adolescent Connectedness includes the subscales to be used in this study: connectedness to friends (end with #2), school (end with #6), teachers (end with #8), peers (end with #7), self-in-the-future (end with #9), and parents (end with #4). Responses to each of the subscale items use a five-point, Likert-type scale ranging from 1 to 5, in which: (1) not true at all, (2) not really true, (3) sort of true, (4) true, (5) very true. There is at least one reverse scored item in each subscale. The six items within each of the subscales are averaged to obtain subscale mean scores. The Connectedness to Teachers subscale (items ending in 8) measures adolescents' efforts to get along with teachers and their concerns about earning their teachers' respect and trust. The scales have demonstrated good three-month test-retest reliability, a distinct factor structure replicated across U.S. and International samples, and evidence of convergent and discriminant validity (Karcher & Sass, 2010; Karcher, Holcomb, & Zambrano, 2008). For the full scale and manual, go to www.adolescentconnectedness.com.

2. Spending time with friends is not so important to me.

3. I can name 5 things that my friends like about me.

4. My family has fun together.

6. I work hard at school.

7. My classmates often bother me.

8. I care what my teachers think of me.

9. I will have a good future.

12. I have friends I'm really close to and trust completely.

13. There is not much that is unique or special about me.

14. It is important that my parents trust me.

16. I enjoy being at school.

17. I like pretty much all of the other kids in my grade.

18. I do not get along with some of my teachers.

19. Doing well in school will help me in the future.

22. Spending time with my friends is a big part of my life.

23. I can name 3 things that other kids like about me.

24. I enjoy spending time with my parents.

26. I get bored in school a lot.

27. I like working with my classmates.

28. I want to be respected by my teachers.

29. I do things outside of school to prepare for my future.

32. My friends and I talk openly with each other about personal things.

33. I really like who I am.

34. My parents and I disagree about many things.

36. I do well in school.

37. I get along well with the other students in my classes.

38. I try to get along with my teachers.

39. I do lots of things in school to prepare for my future.

42. I spend as much time as I can with my friends.

43. I have special hobbies, skills, or talents.

44. My parents and I get along well.

46. I feel good about myself when I am at school.

47. I am liked by my classmates.

48. I always try hard to earn my teachers' trust.

49. I think about my future often.

50. I usually like my teachers.

51. The things I have done in the past will help me in the future.

52. My friends and I spend a lot of time talking about things.

53. I have unique interests or skills that make me interesting.

54. I care about my parents very much.

55. What I do now will not affect my future.

56. Doing well in school is important to me.

57. I rarely fight or argue with the other kids at school.

Mentee Presurvey Completed by Teachers

Youth name _____ Date survey completed _____

Circle your response to each question below.

1. What is the grade level in which this student is currently enrolled?

   4th 5th 6th 7th 8th 9th

2. Compared to the other children in your classroom, how well do you feel you know this child?

   Much less A little less About the same A little better Much better

3. Has this student ever repeated a grade?	No	Yes	I don't know
4. Does the student receive any special support during the school day or after school (e.g., mentoring, pull out tutoring, counseling)?	No	Yes	I don't know
5. Does the child have any physical, emotional or mental condition that interferes with or limits his/her ability to do schoolwork at grade level?	No	Yes	I don't know
6. Is the student a Limited English Proficient (LEP) Student?	No	Yes	I don't know
7. Is the student from a single-parent home?	No	Yes	I don't know

Academic performance and class work

The next few questions ask about the child's academic performance and assignments. Please circle one response for each item and note that questions 15–19 ask about work only in the last four weeks. Please rate the child's academic performance in each of these areas using the following scale.

	Below Grade Level	Needs Improvement	Satisfactory	Very Good	Excellent
Academic performance					
8. Reading	1	2	3	4	5
9. Mathematics	1	2	3	4	5
10. Science	1	2	3	4	5
11. Social studies	1	2	3	4	5
12. Oral language	1	2	3	4	5
13. Written language	1	2	3	4	5
14. Overall academic performance	1	2	3	4	5

	Below Grade Level	Needs Improvement	Satisfactory	Very Good	Excellent
Quality of recent work					
15. Correctness of work in the last 4 weeks	1	2	3	4	5
16. Neatness of work in the last 4 weeks	1	2	3	4	5
17. Completeness of work in the last 4 weeks	1	2	3	4	5
18. Number of in-class assignments turned in, in last 4 weeks	1	2	3	4	5
19. Number of homework assignments turned in, last 4 weeks	1	2	3	4	5

Mentee Presurvey Completed by Parents

Please tell us about this student and show us what behaviors or attitudes you would like to see improvements on through his or her involvement in CAMP?

Child _____ School _____ Grade _____ Date _____

Teacher_____ Teacher e-mail _____

Please tell us about this student. CIRCLE the number that best describes how true each statement is about him or her. "How TRUE is each sentence?"

Not at all = 1, Not really = 2, Sort of true = 3, True = 4, Very true = 5

H1.	This child thinks he/she is doing pretty well	1	2	3	4	5
6C.	This child works hard at school	1	2	3	4	5
7C.	This child's classmates often bother him/her	1	2	3	4	5
8C.	This child cares what his/her teachers think of him/her	1	2	3	4	5
H2.	This child is good at getting the things in life that are most important to him/her	1	2	3	4	5
16C.	This child enjoys being at school	1	2	3	4	5
17C.	This child likes most of the other kids at school	1	2	3	4	5
18C.	This child does not get along with some of his/her teachers	1	2	3	4	5
H3.	This child feels he/she is doing just as well as other kids his/her age	1	2	3	4	5
26C.	This child gets bored at school	1	2	3	4	5
27C.	This child likes working with classmates	1	2	3	4	5
28C.	This child wants to be respected by his/her teachers	1	2	3	4	5
H4.	When this child has a problem, he/she comes up with ways to solve it	1	2	3	4	5
36C.	This child currently does well in school	1	2	3	4	5
37C.	This child gets along well with other students in class	1	2	3	4	5
38C.	This child tries to get along with his/her teachers	1	2	3	4	5
H5.	This child thinks the things he/she has done in the past will help him/her in the future	1	2	3	4	5
46C.	This child feels good about him/herself at school	1	2	3	4	5
47C.	This child is liked by other students	1	2	3	4	5
48C.	This child always tries hard to earn his/her teachers' trust	1	2	3	4	5
H6.	Even when others would quit he/she finds ways to solve the problem	1	2	3	4	5
56C.	Doing well in school is important to this child	1	2	3	4	5
57C.	This child rarely fights or argues with other students	1	2	3	4	5
50C.	This child usually likes his/her teachers	1	2	3	4	5

Mentor and Program Connection Scales

Circle the number of the rating you feel is most true.

My Mentor …	No/Never	Sometimes	Often	Always
(1) … understands me well	1	2	3	4
(2) … says good things about me	1	2	3	4
(3) … likes to spend time with me	1	2	3	4
(4) … is rude to me (Filler item to lessen response set)	1	2	3	4
(5) … knows a lot about me	1	2	3	4
(6) … likes how I am in mentoring	1	2	3	4
(7) … asks me questions about me and my life	1	2	3	4
(8) … is disrespectful to me (Filler item)	1	2	3	4
(9) … accepts me for who I am	1	2	3	4
(10) … makes me feel good about who I am	1	2	3	4
(11) … listens to what I have to say	1	2	3	4

About the Program	No/Never	Sometimes	Often	Always
1. I like what we do together	1	2	3	4
2. I get to do things I like to do	1	2	3	4
3. I like coming to meet my mentor	1	2	3	4
4. I learn things about myself from my mentor	1	2	3	4
5. Mentoring is boring	1	2	3	4
6. I enjoy what we do in mentoring	1	2	3	4

Mentor Connection = (1), (2), (3), (5), (6), (7), (9), (10), (11)

Program Connection = 1., 2., 3., 4., 5., 6.

Filler Variables to Avoid Response Set Bias (omitted from all scales = M4, M8)

Mentee Goal-Directed/Growth-Focus Scales

Responses include 1 = is not at all true 2 = not very true, 3 = sort of true, and 4 = very true

1. My mentor and I work on projects together

2. My mentor and I accomplish a lot of things together

3. My mentor and I spend time working on how I can improve as a person

4. My mentor helps me to set and reach goals

5. My mentor and I talk together about how to solve problems

(DuBois, 2012)

Youth Centeredness

Responses include 1 = is not at all true 2 = not very true, 3 = sort of true, and 4 = very true

1. My mentor almost always asks me what I want to do

2. My mentor is always interested in what I want to do

3. My mentor and I like to do a lot of the same things

4. My mentor thinks of fun and interesting things to do

5. My mentor and I do things I really want to do

(Grossman & Johnson, 1999)

Social Support From Mentors [Feeling valued (bv) and being motivated (bm)]

Feel valued by mentor:

1bv   My mentor cares about how well I am doing in school

2bv   My mentor is very sure that I can do well in school and in the future

3bv   My mentor cares about me even when I make mistakes

4bv   My mentor really listens and understands me

5bv   My mentor looks out for me and helps me

6bv   My mentor and I both have fun when we are together

Feel motivated by mentor:

1bm   My mentor gives me useful advise in dealing with my problems

2bm   My mentor has qualities or skills that I'd like to have when I'm older

3bm   I learn how to do things from watching and listening to my mentor

4bm   My mentor introduces me to new ideas, interests, and things to do

5bm   My mentor pushes me to succeed at things I want to do

(DuBois & Hirsch, 1990)

Staff Support and Space and Resources Scales

1. The CAMP Coordinator at my school seems willing to help me
2. The CAMP Coordinator has shared important information with me about my mentee
3. The CAMP Coordinator has given me suggestions on what I can do with my mentee
4. CAMP Coordinator seems truly concerned about how well my match is going
5. At my school, I have easy access to the Activity Logs I complete
6. At my school, I have easy access to games and other activities
7. At my school, I have a satisfactory space to meet with my mentee
8. At my school, I have easy access to resources I can use with my mentee (e.g., college info.)
9. I've had contact with my mentee's teacher(s)
10. I've had contact with my mentee's parent(s) or guardian

(Karcher, 2004)

Mentor Matters Scale

11m   I am important to my mentee:

12m   I am needed by my mentee:

13m   I am missed by my mentee when I am away:

14m   When I talk, my mentee tries to understand what I am saying:

15m   I am interesting to my mentee:

16m   My mentee notices my feelings:

17m   My mentee gives me credit when I do well:

18m   My mentee notices when I am concerned:

19m   I matter to my mentee:

20m   If your mentee made a list of all the things s/he thinks about in a given day where do you think you'd be on her/his list? (enter a number from 1–7, with 1 as the top and 7 as the bottom of the list)

21m   If your mentee made a list of all the things s/he cares about, where do you think you'd be on her/his list? (enter a numbers from 1–7, with 1 as the top and 7 as the bottom of the list)

(Karcher, 2004; Adapted from Marshall, 2002)

Mentor Self-Efficacy Scale

How confident are you in your:	Not at All Confident	Somewhat Confident	Very Confident	Extremely Confident
a. Ability to provide friendship to a Little Brother/Sister (i.e., a "mentee").	1	2	3	4
b. Ability to be a role model to a mentee.	1	2	3	4
c. Ability to deal with a mentee's behavioral problems.	1	2	3	4
d. Ability to make an appropriate referral for behavioral or emotional problems.	1	2	3	4
e. Knowledge about each of the CAMP Ground Rules.	1	2	3	4
f. Knowledge about the goals of CAMP.	1	2	3	4
g. Knowledge about the role of CAMP staff.	1	2	3	4
h. Ability to provide emotional support to a mentee.	1	2	3	4
i. Ability to help a mentee with school work.	1	2	3	4
j. Ability to help a mentee understand and feel good about what it means to be male/female.	1	2	3	4
k. Ability to help a mentee understand and feel good about his/her racial or ethnic group.	1	2	3	4
l. Ability to help a mentee feel good about the contributions of people of his/her gender in this society.	1	2	3	4
m. Ability to help a mentee feel good about the contributions of people of his/her same race or ethnic group.	1	2	3	4
n. Ability to help a mentee feel good about him/herself.	1	2	3	4
o. Ability to help a mentee establish positive relationships with family members.	1	2	3	4
p. Ability to help a mentee establish positive relationships with adults outside his/her family.	1	2	3	4
q. Ability to help a mentee establish positive relationships with peers.	1	2	3	4
r. Ability to help a mentee participate in appropriate social activities.	1	2	3	4
s. Ability to help a mentee adjust to the school environment.	1	2	3	4

(Parra, DuBois, Neville, Pugh-Lilly, & Pavinelli, 2002)

Mentor Outcome Scale: Academic/School Self-Esteem

Responses include 1 = strongly disagree, 2 = disagree, 3 = agree, and 4 = strongly agree

1.	I am as popular with kids my own age as I want to be.	SD	D	A	SA
2.	I am as good a student as I would like to be.	SD	D	A	SA
3.	I am happy about how much my family likes me.	SD	D	A	SA
4.	I am happy with the way I look.	SD	D	A	SA
5.	I am as good at sports/physical activities as I want to be.	SD	D	A	SA
6.	I am as successful as I want to be at extra-curricular activities (music/arts/clubs/organizations/hobbies).*See note at bottom of page.	SD	D	A	SA
7.	I am happy with the way I can do most things.	SD	D	A	SA
8.	I am as good as I want to be at making new friends.	SD	D	A	SA
9.	I am doing as well on school work as I would like to.	SD	D	A	SA
10.	I am too much trouble to my family.	SD	D	A	SA
11.	I like my body just the way it is.	SD	D	A	SA
12.	I wish I was better at sports/physical activities.	SD	D	A	SA
13.	I wish I did better at extracurricular activities (music/arts/clubs/organizations/hobbies).*	SD	D	A	SA
14.	I sometimes think I am a failure (a "loser").	SD	D	A	SA
15.	I have as many close friends as I would like to have.	SD	D	A	SA
16.	I am good enough at math.	SD	D	A	SA
17.	I get in trouble too much at home.	SD	D	A	SA
18.	I feel good about my height and weight.	SD	D	A	SA
19.	I feel OK about how well I do when I participate in sports/physical activities.	SD	D	A	SA
20.	I feel OK about how well I do when I participate in extracurricular activities (music/arts/clubs/organizations/hobbies).*	SD	D	A	SA
21.	I am happy with myself as a person.	SD	D	A	SA
22.	I am as well liked by other kids as I want to be.	SD	D	A	SA
23.	I am as good at reading and writing as I want to be.	SD	D	A	SA
24.	I feel OK about how important I am to my family.	SD	D	A	SA
25.	I wish I looked a lot different.	SD	D	A	SA
26.	I am happy about how many different kinds of				
27.	I am good at (sports/physical activities).	SD	D	A	SA
28.	I am happy about how many different kinds of extracurricular activities (music/arts/clubs/organizations/hobbies) I am good at.*	SD	D	A	SA
29.	I am the kind of person I want to be.	SD	D	A	SA
30.	I feel good about how well I get along with other kids.	SD	D	A	SA

31. I get grades that are good enough for me.	SD	D	A	SA
32. I get along as well as I would like to with my family.				
33. I wish it were easier for me to learn new kinds of sports/physical activities.	SD	D	A	SA
34. I wish it were easier for me to learn new things in extracurricular activities (music/arts/clubs/organizations/hobbies).*	SD	D	A	SA
35. I often feel ashamed of myself.	SD	D	A	SA
36. I wish my friends liked me more than they do.	SD	D	A	SA
37. I feel OK about how good of a student I am.	SD	D	A	SA
38. My family pays enough attention to me.	SD	D	A	SA
39. I participate in as many different kinds of sports/physical activities as I want to.	SD	D	A	SA
40. I participate in as many extracurricular activities (music/arts/clubs/organizations/hobbies) as I want to.*	SD	D	A	SA
41. I like being just the way I am.	SD	D	A	SA
42. I feel good about how much my friends like my ideas.	SD	D	A	SA
43. I do as well on tests in school as I want to.	SD	D	A	SA
44. I am happy with how much my family loves me.	SD	D	A	SA
45. I am as good a person as I want to be.	SD	D	A	SA
46. I feel OK about how much other kids like doing things with me.	SD	D	A	SA
47. I get too many bad grades on my report cards.	SD	D	A	SA
48. I feel good about how much my family cares about my ideas.	SD	D	A	SA
49. I wish I had more to be proud of.	SD	D	A	SA

*Please do *not* include sports/physical activities when responding to questions about extracurricular activities; that is, think about extracurricular activities other than sports/physical activities.

(Dubois, Felner, Brand, & Phillips, 1996)

Mentee Outcome Scale: Misconduct

Responses include:

1 = I have never done this

2 = I have done this, but not in the last three months

3 = I did it one to two times in the last three months

4 = I did it three to four times in the last three months

5 = I did it five or more times in the last three months

1. Broken something on purpose.
2. Gotten into a fight at school.
3. Had a fight or argument with your parents.
4. Lied to your parents about something important.
5. Taken something on purpose that didn't belong to you.
6. Gotten into a fight in your neighborhood.
7. Taken something from a store without paying for it.
8. Given a teacher a hard time.
9. Had to have your parents come to school about a problem.
10. Done something your parents told you not to do.

(Brown, Clasen, & Eicher, 1986)

Mentor-Mentee Interaction Checklist (Optional)

Responses include 0 = none, 1 = very little, 2 = some, 3 = a lot, 4 = most

Mentors will describe the content of their interactions and discussions with their mentees using a form provided by staff that lists many common activities engaged in during school-based mentoring. The interactions tallied are the same ones as examined in an earlier study (DuBois, Neville, Parra, & Pugh-Lilly, 2002) that found that particular mentoring interactions and discussion content were highly predictive of whether or not mentees came to see their mentors as "significant adults" in later life. Using DuBois, Neville, et al.'s scales, a checklist was created that program site coordinators' have mentors complete after each meeting or monthly. Prescriptive/ Instrumental activities will include discussion of youth's behavior, activities related to homework or schoolwork, and discussion or participation in prevention curricula activities, such as skill building exercises. Developmental/ Psychosocial activities will include discussion of social issues, casual conversation, recreational activities (like sports), game play, and mentor listening to the mentee talk or learning about his or her life (e.g., struggles or successes). There also is space for mentors to write additional activities not listed. These data are entered into a database each month. At the end of the evaluation, the additional activities reported by the mentors will be coded by two raters as either prescriptive, developmental, or ambiguous, based on the definitions provided by Morrow and Styles (1995), will be used as indicators of either the developmental or prescriptive latent factors.

1. Tutoring/homework (helped with reading, library, computer work, etc.)?
2. Sports or athletics (basketball, soccer, catch, etc.)?
3. Creative activities (drawing, arts & crafts, reading and writing for fun, photography, etc.)?
4. Indoor games (board games, cards, chess, puzzles, computer games, etc.)?
5. Talking about your Little's academic issues (e.g., grades, schoolwork, testing)?
6. Talking about your Little's behavior (detention, misbehavior)?
7. Talking about attendance, staying in school, the importance of school?
8. Talking about the future (high school, college, career, goals, dreams, etc.)?
9. Casual conversations (sports, weekend activities, holiday plans)?
10. Talking about social issues (current events/news, poverty, crime, religion, race issues, etc.)?
11. Talking about your Little's friends?
12. Talking about your Little's teachers?
13. Talking about your Little's family?
14. Talking about your Little's romantic friend?
15. Listening and learning (Little's hobbies, interests, and feelings)?

(Karcher, 2004; Karcher, Herrera, & Hansen, 2010)

REFERENCES

Barone, D.F., Hutchings, P.S., Kimmel, H.J., Traub, H.L., Cooper, J.T., & Marshall, C.M. (2005). Increasing empathic accuracy through practice and feedback in a clinical interviewing course. *Journal of Social and Clinical Psychology, 24*(2), 156–171.

Brown, B.B., Clasen, D.R., & Eicher, S.A. (1986). Perceptions of peer pressure, peer conformity dispositions, and self-reported behavior among adolescents. *Developmental Psychology, 22*(4), 521–530.

Cain, J., & Jolliff, B. (1998). *Teamwork & teamplay.* Dubuque, IA: Kendall/Hunt.

Cooper, C.R. (1999). Multiple selves, multiple worlds: Cultural perspectives on individuality and connectedness in adolescent development. *Cultural Processes in Child Development, 29,* 25–57.

Cooper, C.R., Grotevant, H.D., & Condon, S.M. (1983). Individuality and connectedness in the family as a context for adolescent identity formation and role-taking skill. *New Directions for Child Development, 22,* 43–59.

Crandall, J.E. (1991). A scale for social interest. *Individual Psychology, 47*(1), 106–114.

Dishion, T.J., McCord, J., & Poulin, F. (1999). When interventions harm: Peer groups and problem behavior. *American Psychologist, 54*(9), 755–764.

Dodge, K.A., Dishion, T.J., & Lansford, J.E. (Eds.). (2006). *Deviant peer influences in programs for youth: Problems and solutions.* New York, NY: Guilford.

DuBois, D.L. (2013). Program evaluation. In D.L. DuBois & M.J. Karcher (Eds.), *Handbook of youth mentoring.* Thousand Oaks, CA: Sage.

DuBois, D.L., Felner, R.D., Brand, S., & Phillips, R.S. (1996). Early adolescent self-esteem: A developmental-ecological framework and assessment strategy. *Journal of Research on Adolescence, 6*(4), 543–579.

DuBois, D.L., & Hirsch, B.J. (1990). School and neighborhood friendship patterns of Blacks and Whites in early adolescence. *Child Development, 61*(2), 524–536.

DuBois, D.L., Holloway, B.E., Valentine, J.C., & Cooper, H. (2002). Effectiveness of mentoring programs for youth: A meta-analytic review. *American Journal of Community Psychology, 30*(2), 157–197.

DuBois, D.L., Neville, H.A., Parra, G.R., & Pugh-Lilly, A.O. (2002). Testing a new model of mentoring. *New Directions for Youth Development, 93,* 21–57.

DuBois, D.L., Portillo, N., Rhodes, J.E., Silverthorn, N., & Valentine, J.C. (2011).How effective are mentoring programs of youth? A systematic assessment of the evidence. *Psychological Science in the Public Interest, 12*(2), 57–91.

Durlak, J., & DuPre, E. (2008). Implementation matters: A review of research on the influence of implementation on program outcomes and the factors affecting implementation. *American Journal of Community Psychology, 41*(3), 327–350.

Durlak, J., Weissberg, R., & Pachan, M. (2010). A meta-analysis of after-school programs that seek to promote personal and social skills in children and adolescents. *American Journal of Community Psychology, 45*(3), 294–309.

Erikson, E.H. (1950). *Childhood and society.* New York, NY: W.W. Norton.

Erikson, E.H. (1995). *A way of looking at things: Selected papers from 1930 to 1980.* New York, NY: W.W. Norton.

Erikson, J.M. (1988). *Wisdom and the senses: The way of creativity.* New York, NY: W.W. Norton.

Fluegelman, A. (1976). *The new games book.* Garden City, NY: Dolphin Books/Doubleday.

Forbess-Greene, S. (1983). *Encyclopedia of icebreakers: Structured activities that warm-up, motivate, challenge, acquaint, and energize.* San Diego, CA: University Associates.

Garmezy, N. (1981). Children under stress: Perspectives on antecedents and correlates of vulnerability and resistance to psychopathology. In A.I. Rabin, J. Arnoff, M. Barclay & R.A. Zucker (Eds.), *Further explorations in personality.* New York, NY: Wiley Interscience.

Grossman, J.B. (2005). Evaluating mentoring programs. In D.L. DuBois & M.J. Karcher (Eds.), *Handbook of youth mentoring* (pp. 251–265). Thousand Oaks, CA: Sage.

Grossman, J.B., & Johnson, A. (1999). Assessing the effectiveness of mentoring programs. In J.B. Grossman (Ed.), *Contemporary issues in mentoring* (pp. 48–65). Philadelphia, PA: Public/Private Ventures.

Grossman, J.B., & Rhodes, J.E. (2002). The test of time: Predictors and effects of duration in youth mentoring relationships. *American Journal of Community Psychology, 30*(2), 199–219.

Grossman, J.B., & Tierney, J.P. (1998). Does mentoring work? An impact study of the Big Brothers Big Sisters Program. *Evaluation Review, 22*(3), 403–426.

Hamilton, M.A., & Hamilton, S.F. (2005). Work and service-learning. In D.L. DuBois & M.J. Karcher (Eds.), *Handbook of youth mentoring* (pp. 348–363). Thousand Oaks, CA: Sage.

Hamilton, S.F., & Hamilton, M.A. (1992). Mentoring programs: Promise and paradox. *Phi Delta Kappan, 73*(7), 546–550.

Hansen, K. (2006). *BBBS Jack-in-the-Box Partnership report: Summary statistics for the Jack-in-the-Box High School Bigs pilot program for school year 2001–2002.* Philadelphia, PA: Big Brothers Big Sisters of America.

Herrera, C., Grossman, J.B., Kauh, T.J., Feldman, A.F., McMaken, J., & Jucovy, L.Z. (2007). *Big Brothers Big Sisters school-based mentoring impact study.* Philadelphia, PA: Public/Private Ventures.

Herrera, C., Kauh, T.J., Cooney, S.M., Grossman, J.B., & McMaken, J. (2008). *High school students as mentors: Findings from the Big Brothers Big Sisters school-based mentoring impact study.* Philadelphia, PA: Public/Private Ventures.

Ikard, S.S. (2001). Peer mentoring as a method to enhance moral reasoning among high school adolescents. *Dissertation Abstracts International: Section A. Humanities and Social Sciences, 62*(03), 922.

Ivey, A.E. (1986). *Developmental therapy.* San Francisco, CA: Jossey-Bass.

Karcher, M.J. (2004). *The Study of Mentoring in the Learning Environment (SMILE): Year 1 results.* Unpublished manuscript, University of Texas at San Antonio.

Karcher, M.J. (2005a). Mentee/mentor termination ritual. In *How to build a successful mentoring program using the Elements of Effective Practice: A step-by-step tool kit for program managers* (pp. 157–159). Retrieved from MENTOR website: http://www.mentoring.org/downloads/mentoring_413.pdf

Karcher, M.J. (2005b). The effects of school-based developmental mentoring and mentors' attendance on mentees' self-esteem, behavior, and connectedness. *Psychology in the Schools, 42*(1), 65–77.

Karcher, M.J. (2005c). Cross-age peer mentoring. In D.L. DuBois, & M.J. Karcher (Eds.), *Handbook of youth mentoring* (pp. 266–285). Thousand Oaks, CA: Sage.

Karcher, M.J. (2006). What happens when high school mentors don't show up? In L. Golden & P. Henderson (Eds.), *Case studies in school counseling* (pp. 44–53). Alexandria, VA: ACA Press.

Karcher, M.J. (2007). Cross-age peer mentoring. *Youth Mentoring: Research in Action, 1*(7), 3–17.

Karcher, M.J. (2008). The Cross-Age Mentoring Program (CAMP): A developmental intervention for promoting students' connectedness across grade levels. *Professional School Counseling, 12*(2), 137–143.

Karcher, M.J. (2009). Increases in academic connectedness and self-esteem among high school students who serve as cross-age peer mentors. *Professional School Counseling, 12*(4), 292–299.

Karcher, M.J., & Benne, K. (2008). Erik and Joan Eriksons' approach to human development in counseling. In K. Kraus (Ed.), *Lifespan development in action: A case study approach for counseling professionals* (pp. 199–238). Indianapolis, IN: Lahaska Press.

Karcher, M.J., Davidson, A., Rhodes, J.E., & Herrera, C. (2010). Pygmalion in the program: The role of teenage peer mentors' attitudes in shaping their mentees' outcomes. *Applied Developmental Science, 14*(4), 1–16.

Karcher, M.J., Davis, C.I., & Powell, B. (2002). The effects of developmental mentoring on connectedness and academic achievement. *School Community Journal, 12*(2), 36–50.

Karcher, M.J., Herrera, C., & Hansen, K. (2010). "I dunno, what do you wanna do?" Testing a framework to guide mentor training and activity selection. *New Directions in Youth Development, 126,* 51–70.

Karcher, M.J., Holcomb, M., & Zambrano, E. (2008). Measuring adolescent connectedness: A guide for school-based assessment and program evaluation. In H.L.K. Coleman & C. Yeh (Ed.), *Handbook of school counseling* (pp. 649–669). Mahwah, NJ: Lawrence Erlbaum.

Karcher, M.J., & Judson, B. (in press). *The Cross-Age Mentoring Program (CAMP) for children with adolescent mentors: Connectedness curriculum.* San Antonio, TX: Developmental Press.

Karcher, M.J., Kuperminc, G., Portwood, S., Sipe, C., & Taylor, A. (2006). Mentoring programs: A framework to inform program development, research, and evaluation. *Journal of Community Psychology, 34*(6), 709–725.

Karcher, M.J., & Lindwall, J. (2003). Social interest, connectedness, and challenging experiences: What makes high school mentors persist? *Journal of Individual Psychology, 59*(3), 293–315.

Karcher, M.J., & Nakkula, M.J. (2010). Youth mentoring with a balanced focus, shared purpose, and collaborative interactions. *New Directions in Youth Development, 126,* 13–32.

Karcher, M.J., Nakkula, M.J., & Harris, J. (2005). Developmental mentoring match characteristics: The effects of mentors' efficacy and mentees' emotional support seeking on the perceived quality of mentoring relationships. *Journal of Primary Prevention, 26*(2), 93–110.

Karcher, M.J. & Sass, D. (2010). A multicultural assessment of adolescent connectedness: Testing measurement invariance across gender and ethnicity. *Journal of Counseling Psychology, 57*(3), 274–289.

Kegan, R. (1982). *The evolving self.* Cambridge, MA: Harvard University Press.

Keller, T.E., & Pryce, J.M. (2010). Mutual but unequal: Mentoring as a hybrid of familiar relationship roles. *New Directions for Youth Development, 126,* 33–50.

Kohut, H. (1977). *The restoration of the self.* New York, NY: International Universities Press.

Langhout, R.D., Rhodes, J.E., & Osborne, L.N. (2004). An exploratory study of youth mentoring in an urban context: Adolescents' perceptions of relationship styles. *Journal of Youth and Adolescence, 33*(4), 293–306.

Larose, S., Cyrenne, D., Garceau, O., Brodeur, P., & Tarabulsy, G.M. (2010). The structure of effective academic mentoring in late adolescence. *New Directions for Youth Development, 126,* 123–140.

Marshall, S. (2002). Do I matter? Construct validation of adolescents' perceived mattering to parents and friends. *Journal of Adolescence, 24*(4), 473–490.

Morrow, K.V., & Styles, M.B. (1995). *Building relationships with youth in program settings: A study of Big Brothers/Big Sisters.* Philadelphia, PA: Public/Private Ventures.

Nakkula, M.J., & Harris, J.T. (2010). Beyond the dichotomy of work and fun: Measuring the thorough interrelatedness of structure and quality in youth mentoring relationships. *New Directions for Youth Development, 126,* 71–87.

Parra, G.R., DuBois, D.L., Neville, H.A., Pugh-Lilly, A.O., & Pavinelli, N. (2002). Mentoring relationships for youth: Investigation of a process-oriented model. *Journal of Community Psychology, 30*(4), 367–388.

Ratey, J., & Hagerman, E. (2008). *Spark: The revolutionary new science of exercise and the brain.* New York, NY: Little, Brown.

Rhodes, J.E. (2002). *Stand by me: The risks and rewards of mentoring today's youth.* Cambridge, MA: Harvard University Press.

Rohnke, K. (1989). *Cowstails and cobras II.* Dubuque, IA: Kendall/Hunt.

Selman, R.L. (1980). *The growth of interpersonal understanding: Developmental and clinical analyses.* New York, NY: Academic Press.

Selman, R.L., & Schultz, L.H. (1990). *Making a friend in youth: Developmental theory and pair therapy.* Chicago, IL: University of Chicago Press.

Smith, C., Peck, S., Denault, A.-S., Blazevski, J., & Akiva, T. (2010). Quality at the point of service: Profiles of practice in after-school settings. *American Journal of Community Psychology, 45*(3), 358–369.

Stoltz, A.D. (2006). The relationship between peer mentoring program participation and successful transition to high school. *Dissertation Abstracts International: Section A. Humanities and Social Sciences, 66*(07), 2494.

Sullivan, H.S. (1953). *The interpersonal theory of psychiatry.* New York, NY: W.W. Norton.

Vygotsky, L.S. (1978). *Mind in society: The development of higher psychological processes* (M. Cole, F. John-Steiner, S. Scribner, & E. Souberman, Trans.). Cambridge, MA: Harvard University Press.

Wampold, B.E. (2001). *The great psychotherapy debate: Models, methods, and findings.* Mahwah, NJ: Lawrence Erlbaum.

www.ingramcontent.com/pod-product-compliance
Lightning Source LLC
Chambersburg PA
CBHW082356270326
41935CB00013B/1646